CONTENTS

This book is dedicated to my father,
without whom truly none of this would be possible,

to my mother,
without whom I wouldn't be here at all,

and to Tanya ("The Admiral"),
for the infinite patience she's sure she has.

Love you, Babe.

〜

Connect at
HowNotToSail.com

Second Edition–2020
Copyright ©2019, 2020 by Bradford Rogers

ISBN 9781079085204

Worldsongs Media
4062 Peachtree Rd. NE #A-313
Brookhaven, GA 30319

U.S. trade bookstores and wholesalers:
Please contact bradford@bradfordrogers.com

DISCLAIMER

Do NOT try any of the stupid stuff described in this book.

*Doing so could result in injury to you and your boat,
or other people and their boats.*

*(Also, do not read this book if you have trouble
recognizing irony or sarcasm. Just sayin'.)*

NOTE:

If you're an astute observer, you'll notice that the first paragraph of
each chapter seems a little...backwards.

In most cases, this serves to illustrate some popular misconception
about owning and enjoying a cruising sailboat.

In other cases, it's just because the author's a little backwards himself.

ANOTHER LIFE RUINED...

I've known Bradford Rogers for a few years now, and I gotta tell ya, when it comes to sailing he is not the brightest bulb in the pack!

Sailing with Bradford keeps you feeling like a long tailed cat in a room full of rocking chairs. Even if you make it back to the dock, you are still wondering just how you made it back safe! If there is anything to be gleaned from this book it is how not to sail.

Hey, that's the name of the book!! What a kewl discovery!

Bob Bitchin
Publisher & Janitorial Assistant
Latitudes & Attitudes

THIS BOOK IS NOT ABOUT SAILING.

It's a tough job, but somebody's gotta do it. Might as well be YOU, right?

I'm not an expert sailor. I could have called this book "How Not To Cruise."

Like many cruisers, I use the engine a lot. In fact, my handy

Google spreadsheet says that 75% of my time underway has been under power.

Half the time, I'm just motoring. Another 25% of the time, I'm motorsailing. (And then there's that blissful other 25% of the time...)

Come to think of it, I guess a lot of cruisers would say I'm not a real cruiser, either. I don't think I've attended a potluck yet, or called in to a radio net. We don't cook a whole lot on board. I'm not even all that sociable.

(For example, I don't particularly want you anchoring right next to me in a secluded anchorage and sharing your choice of music with me. I was actually thinking about naming my boat *Do Not Disturb*. Hmmm...maybe I should rethink my approach here.)

Anyway, I'm not saying I'm an expert in how to do things right on a boat.

I haven't traveled the world. My cruising so far has been between St. Pete, the Florida Gulf Coast, the Keys, and Cuba. I don't live aboard *Jacie Sails* (yet!).

I've even been known to pay for a marina slip when a perfectly good hot, rolly anchorage is available.

What I have done, though, is sail — er, cruise — over 6,000 miles in the last few years, and gained a ton of valuable experience in what **not** to do.

And in that area, I'm an expert.

So if you're thinking of buying a sailboat and going cruising but you're worried about screwing up, fear not. I've made plenty of mistakes aboard *Jacie Sails*, and I'm still alive to tell about 'em.

I hope this book will light in you that fire to go traveling about in your own boat, enable you to avoid some of the stupid mistakes I've made, and give you the *chutzpah* to overcome unnecessary fears.

After all, if I can do it, so can any reasonably sentient human. As I say on the *How Not To Sail podcast*,

"What could possibly go wrong?"

∾

MORE How Not To Sail...

In case you want to explore further and keep up with the latest dumb things I've done, I also have a podcast that a few folks seem to like. You can find it right here on my website,

HowNotToSail.com

...as well as on Apple (iTunes) Podcasts, Google Podcasts, Spotify, Pandora, RadioPublic, you name it.

There's also the YouTube channel,

YouTube.com/HowNotToSail

And I welcome you to join me in the private Facebook group. (Don't forget to answer the membership questions if you want to come aboard!)

Facebook.com/groups/HowNotToSail

But getting back to that "cruising problem" you're developing...

Let's go find that perfect boat, shall we?

PART I

THE BOAT

1

FINDING THE PERFECT BOAT

Don't give up! Keep searching for that perfect boat...it's out there. No, really!

I'm sure that somewhere in the world is a boat that you can afford that meets every single criterion on your list: Roomy inside, but comfortable and safe at sea. The perfect layout and galley. Tons of water and fuel tankage. The perfect rig. Just be patient and don't settle for anything less than your dream boat.

You may miss out on some great experiences in the meantime, but that's just the way it goes.

~

I have a certain friend, who shall remain nameless (Todd, you know who you are!), who has a lot more capacity for trivia than I do.

My friend was interested in buying a sailboat, and to that end created a spreadsheet comparing various models, with specs like fuel and water capacity, "comfort ratio," and various other notes, like whether the traveler was located on the cabin top or on the companionway step.

He was able to quote to me a number of things about my boat that I didn't even know.

Halloween 2012. Blackbeard.

I arrived at my boat purchase via a slightly different methodology: I dressed up as Blackbeard for Halloween, and a boat fell into my lap just a couple of days later.

Good Luck

Our friend Captain Elmore had looked at a 1983 Hunter Cherubini on Lake Lanier, near Atlanta. He swore Tanya to secrecy until he had a chance to decide if he wanted to buy the boat, then named *Bond's Voyage*.

Fortunately for me, Captain Elmore's wife Susan didn't enjoy the breezy test drive, so he gave Tanya the go-ahead to clue me in.

At first, I wasn't as interested in the opportunity as The Admiral was. ("The Admiral" would be my First Mate in life, Tanya.) I had my eye set on an *ocean boat*, not a lake boat. But Captain Elmore's recommendation and Tanya's enthusiasm were enough to get me to the lake on a Saturday to take a look.

I'd been reading about Morgans, Cape Dorys, Tartans, Endeavors and the like. (Even Westsails.) And of course, I'd been drooling over all the latest Beneteaus, Jeanneaus, and Island Packets. I was even hot for a little swing keel number for a minute. But all of these new boats were beyond my budget.

I thought about getting a loan, but thankfully rejected that idea in a fit of sanity. It may have had something to do with reading *Sensible Cruising*, or one of the many other books warning against such foolishness.

I'd looked at a few sailboats around St. Pete, but none of them in my price range really did a lot for me.

Fortunately, I wasn't attached to a particular brand or model. I just wanted something that could go out on the ocean, and that I could afford.

And then *Jacie Sails* came along.

The Test Drive

I didn't know that to expect when we parked on the hilltop at Sunrise Cove marina and walked down the hillside to the docks. But there in slip J28 was a clean, well-kept white boat with blue trim.

Well, okay, like ninety percent of fiberglass boats are white with blue trim. But that's another story.

The inside was tidy. Thomas and Lisa had been meticulous in their upkeep. Thomas had served in the military, and clearly both "parents" were intent on keeping their stuff up to snuff. And since the boat had been in fresh, temperate Georgia water for years, corrosion and rust were about zero.

(I have to admit to you here, I have this "ability" to zone out on details and information when it suits me. My assessment of the boat then known as *Bond's Voyage* was, "Yep, neat, tidy. Looks good to me.")

She was a cutter, which was fine. I had envisioned a sloop; but hey, what's an extra sail here and there, anyway? At least it had just one mast. Those ketches and yawls and schooners looked a little complicated for sailing singlehanded, and I knew I planned to do some of that.

(Of course, all kind of famous singlehanders sail ketches and the like, but those rigs looked intimidating to me.)

We took *Bond's Voyage* out for a spin. I was on overload, making sure to ignore all manner of details and information. The usual goofy grin on my face became a painfully wide grin. I'm sure I managed to sound like I was having a conversation, but my mind was far away in the Gulf of Mexico and the Caribbean. I'm not sure if I'd decided to buy her yet, but the fat lady was warming up in the green room, as they say.

We brought her back to the dock and chatted a little more about something or other. I had no idea what to look for as far as potential defects, so my "survey" consisted of snapping a smartphone picture of the keel bolts and sending it to Captain Elmore and also Captain Mitch, neither of whom who saw anything amiss with the keel bolts.

To Buy Or Not To Buy

It was up to me now. Thomas and Lisa had another appointment the next day with a potential buyer.

I weighed my decision carefully.

(Okay, I didn't really. I talked to Captain Elmore and Captain Mitch, who both thought that for the asking price, I should have a nice boat to meet my needs; and that I could make all manner of modifications to suit me and still be way under the cost of a new boat.)

"Sure, what the hell!"

I showed up the next day, checkbook in hand, like a damned idiot. Thomas and Lisa were asking $25,000. I knew my dad wouldn't be proud unless I haggled a little, so I offered $24,000 on the spot.

Done! I was now the proud owner of a nine ton, thirty-seven foot boat.

Holy Crap... I just bought a boat!

And the rest, as they say...

You know how they say the two happiest days of a man's life are when he buys his boat and sells his boat? Well, I can say I'm not remotely ready for that second day yet.

And I've had a helluva time sailing around the Gulf Coast, Florida Keys and Cuba already. To steal part of a quote from Bob Bitchin, I highly recommend it.

I shipped the boat down to Florida, renamed her *Jacie Sails*, and invested a large quantity of "boat bucks" on upgrades, just as my friends envisioned. (All the through-hulls had those damned cheap garden hose gate valves instead of proper through hulls. We fixed that asap.)

Now, if you've already spotted a number of rookie mistakes, good on ya!

I don't recommend at all buying a boat without having a survey done. And that goes double if she's gonna be on salt water!

I've never been much on shopping, and I usually have to force myself to do research on purchases and things. I don't recommend that, either.

But I do gently suggest that if you plan to go cruising before you're too old to crank a winch, you'd be wise to keep an eye out for a boat that may not quite have the layout or rig or specs you had in mind, but that you may just learn to love.

2

THE BIGGER, THE BETTER

THIS ONE SHOULD BE OBVIOUS. Of course you want to get the biggest boat you can almost afford. They're so much more comfortable, and you can't have all your grand offshore adventures in a puny little boat. Let's face it, bigger sailboats are just cooler.

≈

Well, okay, bigger sailboats are cooler...in a way. Frankly, though, I've learned to appreciate the beauty of a smaller sailboat properly set up and maintained.

First of all, there's the economic aspect: You can't enjoy your boat as much (or as often) if you're busy earning those "fun tickets" to pay off a large loan.

And it's not just the cost of the boat itself that swells up like a hammer-struck thumb when you get a bigger boat. The insurance cost goes up, too. And the cost of your boat slip, at home port or when traveling, goes by the foot.

There's a not-so-obvious cost increase, too. A bigger boat means more force on the rigging and everything else — meaning bigger, stronger, more expensive winches, standing and running rigging, and I don't know what all.

And let's talk about safety. In 1982, Tom McClean crossed the Atlantic in *Giltspur, a 7'9" sailboat.* (Tom had a small boat, but some large *cojones.*) Maybe you don't want something quite that small to cruise in. But maybe you don't need a fifty footer, either.

There are sixty-foot sailboats that shouldn't be in the water; and there are twenty-eight foot boats that are blue water-ready. Your safety at sea has more to do with construction, design and maintenance than it does with size.

Stout rigging, inspected regularly, is a good thing. So is a full keel, or at least a skeg-hung rudder, to protect your rudder in case you run over a whale, or a log, or a floating container or something. (*Jacie Sails* does *not* have such things, but that ain't stopping me! They never did say I was all that bright.)

In some ways a smaller boat is actually *safer*, especially if you're a cruising couple or sailing singlehanded — or are not as strong as you think. The higher forces that act on a larger boat require not only beefed-up hardware, but also can make it tough — if not impossible — to do essential things when it's ugly out there. That is a hugely important deal. Even when things aren't actually *unsafe*, they can be no fun if your boat's hard to manage.

Just like there are crazy sons of bitches that have sailed across oceans in micro-yachts, there are others, like Alain Colas, who (as far as I know) holds the record for the largest singlehanded sailor. (The boat, not the guy...the boat being 236 feet in length.)

I think the sweet spot is somewhere in between.

Jacie Sails is a 37' sailboat, and I think that's about as large as I'd want for singlehanding. I feel great about *Jacie* but if I can still sail her singlehanded when I'm sixty, then I'll be a sixty-year-old you don't wanna mess with.

Some say the weight (displacement) of the boat is more important than length in deciding how suitable the boat is for single handing, with nine tons being the upper limit — which, coincidentally, is exactly what *Jacie Sails* displaces.

Jacie Sails at Cabbage Key. Just big enough.

My sense is that 28' is about the minimum-sized sailboat you'd want for comfortable cruising, and (maybe I'm prejudiced) I'd put 37' and 9 tons at the top end of the range.

But as Don Casey and Lew Hackler say in *Sensible Cruising: The Thoreau Approach*, the boat you want is the one you can afford without debt, that can get you to where you want to go...*now*.

In fact, a lot of smart folks say that. But I highly recommend *Sensible Cruising* as a good dose of reality before you go and basically take out a second mortgage.

(Casey and Hackler also have a lot of other cool ideas, and I love the whole Essentialism of their approach. And while we're on books for cruisers...*Essentialism*, by Greg McKeown, was a real whack on the side of the head for me.)

So if you've got the cruising bug (or think you do), be realistic about what size boat you can afford and can operate without drama. You'll save money up front, save a ton of expenses, possibly save your back (or your marriage), and dispense with a whole lotta worrying.

And sure, a big boat is kinda cool. But all that extra dough you save on a reasonable-sized vessel can allow you to take your properly outfitted self to a lot of awesome destinations. And that's pretty cool, too.

3

WHO NEEDS AN ENGINE?

HEY, Moitessier didn't have an engine. Why should I? Just think how impressive it'll be when I sail into the marina slip. Plus, I can save all kinds of money on fuel and maintenance.

Sure, I'll admit it. My favorite time on the boat may be that blissful few seconds after I've hoisted the sails, when I ease the throttle off to nothing, turn the key off, and...*ahhhhh!*

Suddenly I realize how loud and vibrate-y it was just a moment before. Now I can hear the hiss of the wake, the gentle flopping of the sails, and the gurgling of the cockpit drains.

At times like these, I start to fancy myself a true descendant of all the great sailors.

Hey, I don't need no steenkin' engine! I'll just sail in and out of the marina. Just wait 'til they get a look a that!

And then sanity kicks in.

The first thing is, I don't actually recommend trying to dock under sail, if any other option is available. For some reason it seems to make harbormasters a little grumpy — possibly because of the large chance you'll damage somebody's expensive yacht with your shenanigans.

I learned (or re-learned) a valuable lesson one time in Sarasota, when *somebody* let the diesel run dry, and we had to take a mooring under sail.

Okay, maybe a couple of lessons.

On the mooring in Sarasota.

The first lesson is: People are idiots.

On our tenth pass or so at the ball (mind you, we weren't making a huge orbit each time), some asshat in a catamaran came surging out of the marina and tried to pick up the ball we'd been circling for ten minutes. He seemed a little vexed when I vehemently waved him off.

The second lesson: *I'm* an idiot.

This was reinforced when, unable to find a mechanic around, we (okay, *I*) decided to leave the mooring under sail and pinch north up Sarasota Bay towards home.

It was then that I was reminded of some basic physics.

A sailboat underway with a sufficient (but not too sufficient) amount of wind coming from the right direction is a beautiful, controllable vessel. But a sailboat just getting underway, or in an insufficient amount of wind, or with the wind on the nose, is a wallowing tub, subject to the mercies of the wind and current.

The same wind that can push or pull the boat forward once properly underway can also, prior to attaining said momentum, push the boat into solid, unforgiving objects. Like rocks, reefs...and other boats.

(I'm grateful to the older couple in the boat with the pirate flag in the Sarasota anchorage for leaping out of their cabin, helping fend of *Jacie Sails*, and not cussing me out for nearly t-boning them. The gentleman even jumped into his dinghy and insisted on retrieving a fender I'd lost in the melee. Clearly they are much more patient than your humble narrator.)

*Any*way, after that debacle, we slowly sailed north up the bay and the narrow ICW beyond. And which way was the wind blowing? You guessed it. From the north. It took hours to make just a few miles, during which we were treated to a number of interesting encounters. (*See* "Species Of ICW Idiots.")

Finally, in Anna Maria Sound, I gave up and called Towboat US. Trying to sail close to the wind through drawbridges along with the Spring Break crowd seemed unwise. And even if we made it through the gauntlet unscathed, it would probably be some time in the middle of the night when we got The Admiral, along with her niece and nephew, back to home port. (They had already been exposed to some new and colorful language during the near t-boning episode and while sailing up the ICW.)

So, um, yeah... Not having an engine ain't all it's cracked up to be. Sure, if you're sailing out in the open ocean and dropping the anchor in an empty bay — and you have either a favorable wind or plenty of time — an engine isn't a *sine qua non*.

But as for me, I usually don't have unlimited time. And if you've sailed much, you know that saying: "Either too much wind, or not enough. But it'll be on the nose.")

And then there's docking. *Don't do it under sail.*

The fact is, you need that iron jenny for docking and undocking, getting through narrow channels and drawbridges, and all sorts of things. And it's darned handy for anchoring and taking a mooring. Your neighbors will thank you.

A reliable engine is also pretty swell when you need to get somewhere faster than that headwind or two knot breeze allows, or when you need to get the heck out of trouble. (Cruise ships and approaching storms come to mind.) You may have the right of way over that supertanker, but that'll be cold comfort when they pry your remains off the bow because you were becalmed in the shipping channel.

It's true that maintaining and repairing the engine can represent a substantial part of the cost of owning a sailboat. (This very morning I sent a check for $374.[50] to a gentleman for aligning my prop shaft and engine. After shelling out about $1,000 for parts and labor for new motor mounts for the same engine.)

It's also true that engines — especially of the diesel variety — are noisy and smelly.

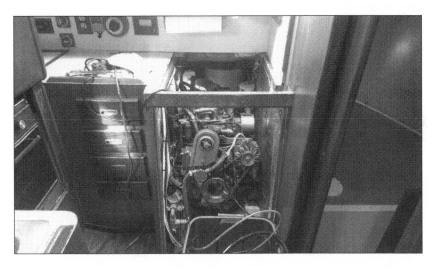

Engine maintenance fun...

When I first got *Jacie Sails*, I used to wonder if we were about to fry the engine or something, every time I happened to motor downwind. (In this case, it was just the exhaust...but check your oil, anyway!)

And engines negate one of the primary benefits of sailing: namely, quiet. After being in possibly one of the loudest bands on the planet, I cherish the quiet. I like to hear the splash of the water and all the little creaks and groans *Jacie* makes on her path through the water. I rarely play music. And since I sail by myself a lot, there's not much conversation, usually.

But for all the noise, fumes, maintenance and expense, it's always gratifying to pull the red throttle lever up, turn that rusty key, press the rubber button in, and hear that sucker rattle into life.

And maybe someday, when I'm much savvier than I am now, I'll sail *Jacie Sails* into her slip.

4

THE DINGHY

OF COURSE you need a worthy dinghy for all of those scuba expeditions you're gonna launch. Plus all those guests and groceries.

❧

So, I went big on my first dinghy. But at least I didn't buy a new one. I went to a place near St. Pete that I found online, and bought a used 10'2" Achilles inflatable with an 8.5 horsepower Yamaha outboard, and got both for around $1,200.

I figured this was about the smallest size that would allow four people aboard if necessary, or several jerrycans of fuel or water, or whatever.

The fellow at the store was obviously sympathetic to cheap — er, thrifty — Florida cruisers, so he wrote up most of the cost of the sale as being the outboard motor.

Why? Because in Florida you have to pay a yearly tax on any motorized dinghy — but the tax is based on the cost of the dinghy itself, not the motor.

You can see why Florida is sometimes referred to as "a sunny place for shady people." (Or maybe that's just Fort Lauderdale.)

When we got back to *Jacie Sails*, we made a discovery: The thing was big.

Jacie Sails is 11.5 feet wide midships, but just a little over 7 feet wide at the stern.

So when we hoisted the "new" dinghy up under the davits, she stuck out from either side, perfect for snagging a piling when coming into or out of a dock...not that that's ever happened.

One good thing about that first dink, which I now refer to as "MJ" after the last part of her registration numbers, is that she was built to go with a good strong motor like the one we got with her.

She had an inflatable floor, which firmed up nicely under pressure, plus an inflatable v-hull. This allowed her to rise up on a plane, which is critical if you want to get from the sailboat to the shore any time this century, while staying relatively dry.

But this robust construction (including a plywood transom, midships seat and aluminum oars), plus the outboard, made MJ *heavy*.

I still host a regular lecture for The Admiral on *Why We Can't Keep The Dinghy And Motor On The Davits While We're At Sea.*

"Why can't we keep the dinghy on there?" she will ask.

"Because it's about to rip the davits off the stern," I'll say.

At this point, she will stare at me pointedly. "I don't think so."

Granted, it's a drag to have to bring the dinghy up from the cabin (where it's taking up valuable space), assemble and inflate it, hoist it over into the water, and wrestle the motor over *Jacie*'s rail before we can explore whatever cool anchorage we just landed in.

One time launching MJ at Longboat Key, I took an impromptu swim when The Admiral and I had a disagreement about who was supposed to be holding the line to keep MJ attached to *Jacie Sails*. Of course, we hadn't attached the motor or the oars yet, so it took me a few minutes to paddle MJ back to the mother ship using one arm, as I lay on the starboard pontoon. I'd taken just enough time to flip off my shoes, but apparently the sight of me in shorts and sock feet, stroking this big inflatable back up-current to *Jacie* was great entertainment for the anchorage.

MJ weighed close to a hundred and fifty pounds with the motor. And that, plus the fact she was wider than the davits, meant that she was next to impossible to secure in place.

In anything other than a flat calm, she would squeal against the stainless uprights of the davits, or get loose and slam into them. I could see the davits flexing and shaking as she bounced around.

There seemed to be nothing I could do. If I tried to secure her with regular lines, she would chafe against them. Bungee cords didn't work either.

MJ's demise began when I towed her from Key West to Fort Myers Beach. I knew that hanging her on the davits wouldn't work, so I attached a dock line to the ring inside her bow, and towed her seventy miles or so with that.

As I should have known, when I got to Fort Myers, the line had chafed away the outer layer of the bow. Duct tape worked to protect that part of the dink, but other injuries followed.

One time I decided to leave MJ on the davits when I went back to Atlanta. Unfortunately, I forgot to pull the drain plug, so in short order she filled up with a hundred pounds of rain water, and the wooden transom pulled away from the inflatable sides.

I got that fixed, but by the time The Admiral and I tried to launch MJ at the Dry Tortugas on our way to Cuba, she was toast.

I found the leak, along the bottom of the dinghy, where it looked like I'd scraped it on something. Some kind folks in the anchorage (and even a couple of the park rangers) lent me some adhesive and various bits of rubber to try to fix it the leak.

But after a day of curing in the sun...it was not to be.

So The Admiral and I made the crossing to Cuba without a dinghy, and I made peace with MJ's passing.

∿

S o now I've bought a smaller dinghy, used of course. It's only 8' 6", and doesn't have the inflatable floor or v-hull. The motor is 2.5 horsepower instead of 8.5. (I did keep the old motor, just in case, but it's way too much for this dinghy, I think.)

It's still a beast to wrestle the new guy from the cabin to the deck to launch. (And this one is made of PVC instead of Hypalon, which means the sun will eat it up even faster than MJ. So I can't keep it hanging on the davits while I go home, either.)

But I think this one will work fine for now. It may be a little underpowered for some tasks, but those will be rare the way we've been cruising since Cuba. And the number of times we've had more that two folks in either dinghy is...zero.

So when it comes to dinghies:

Less is more.

IT MUST BE A "CLASSIC"

DON'T WASTE your time with one of those ugly floating fiberglass bath-tubs. What you want is a classic wooden boat, a stunning vision in teak and brass. After all, you're gonna have an image to maintain!

∾

Let's just say I politely disagree. You can waste a lot of beer money on a "classic" boat.

First of all, as to wooden boats: You couldn't pay me to have one in Florida. Well, unless you're paying me enough to have a full-time maintenance crew.

Wooden boats and warm water go together like Democrats and Republicans. If you dream of warm destinations like the Caribbean, and you're not living aboard with a lot of free time, I don't recommend 'em. Most of the wooden boats in my marina that don't have full-time care look like crap.

I'm talking about the hull here, but my aversion to maintaining wood extends to the topsides as well. Some people (Bob, you know who you are!) actually seem to enjoy varnishing teak and polishing brass.

I do not.

My situation may be different than yours. But then again, it may be similar. I don't live right up the street from my boat — or on it. I have an eight-hour commute to get to *Jacie Sails*. And when I get there, I want to go sailing.

I like the teak handrails on the cabin top (they're handy, too) and the thin teak "eyebrows" above the port lights — it would look weird without those.

But I keep them *au naturel*. I'll put some tung oil or whatever on them periodically, but otherwise I let the sun bleach them gray. The same goes for the companionway step and the few other places above deck where we have wood.

I have a similar *lessez-faire* attitude about boat brands as well.

A lot of folks, when they start the boat-shopping, they only want to look at certain manufacturers. A Beneteau, Oyster, Hylas, or Jeanneau among the newer boats, or maybe a classic Tartan or Cape Dory if you're drooling over the used Boats For Sale pages in *Latitudes & Attitudes*.

Maybe I'm prejudiced here, but I like my 1983 Hunter Cherubini just fine, thank you.

Because of the lack of a full keel or much protection from the rudder, you may not see me crossing the ocean in it. But then again, you just might.

She's taken me 6,000 miles so far without major incident. And I'm not the sharpest tool in the shed when it comes to sailing.

I've grounded a few times. (Okay, as I think Bob Bitchin said, I've seen more bottom than a gynecologist.) I check the oil sporadically. And I haul her out to redo the bottom paint...well, I haven't done that yet. I probably should.

*At this point, my attorney has advised me to point out that you should **not** attempt to cross the ocean in such a sailboat. He also has advised me to point out that you should check your oil regularly, avoid running aground, and get a new coat of bottom paint every couple of years.*

My boat is one of those "production" models that the yachties like to sneer at, but I love her. She's reliable, forgiving, and actually makes pretty good time under most points of sail, with a minimum of fuss.

And to me, at least, she's a beautiful vessel. A little more reminiscent of some kind of escape pod from 2001: A Space Odyssey than a classic schooner or something...but beautiful to my eye.

Even better, I bought her in great condition for the grand total of $24,000.

And that's a lot of money saved for beer — I mean, maintenance.

AUTOHELM IS FOR WIMPS

AUTOHELM IS expensive and prone to issues. And as I've discovered, the yahoos putting it in can even forget to leave enough room for the hydraulic arm and your propane locker to peaceably coexist. And how often are you going to use autohelm anyway? Just save your money for something more useful.

～

Pardon my French here, but autohelm is THE. BEST. FRIGGIN'. INVENTION. EVER.

I think I read somewhere that autohelm was one of the top things to add when refitting your boat. (And I think my friend Captain Mitch told me that, too.) Of course, I didn't believe it.

But 6,000 miles later, I damn sure do. And I get kinda cranky when one of the electronics cables comes loose and I have to actually steer the boat!

You see, with "Otto" keeping you pointed in the direction you're supposed to be heading, you're free to sip a cold beverage and converse with your guests (or yourself)...while of course keeping a regular eye on things like land, shallows, and other boats. (Some people seem to forget this critical last part. (*See "Don't Bore Me With Rules"*).

And while hand steering is plenty fine for racing around the buoys, it gets old pretty fast when you're making the 70-mile leap from Marco Island to Marathon. Or the 190-mile leap from St. Pete to the Dry Tortugas.

Autohelm can be handy in other situations as well. Like the time I was crossing back across the Straits of Florida from Cuba.

The crossing south with The Admiral had been a milk run, of course. The seas were like glass. We made 8 knots motorsailing with the main up, and arrived earlier than we expected.

Then The Admiral had to fly back home and I had to wait a few days to find some "good" weather.

"Good" is a relative thing. 10-foot seas were better than 15-foot seas, but my 14-day allowance from the U.S. was up. So I had to go.

I managed not to chum the waters with my last cuban meal. But just barely.

By halfway through the 14-hour crossing, I had developed a routine: Stand at the helm for a few minutes, or as long as I could stand it without heaving. Then go sit in the leeward (lower) corner of the cockpit next to the cabin, staring up at the oncoming waves as they blocked out the rising moon, until that position made me nauseous as well. Then back to the helm again.

I kept the main up and the engine on all the way to Key West. My left foot developed blisters from standing at a 30° angle all night.

When I stood at the helm, I was not holding on to the wheel. Oh, no. That thing was jerking around way too much for my taste. No, I was holding on to the curved steel tube at the top of the pedestal, while "Otto" drove the boat like a champ all night and into the morning.

That, my friends, is the beauty of autohelm.

TROUBLESHOOTING: IT'S NEVER SOMETHING OBVIOUS

I CAN SAVE you a lot of time here: Don't waste time checking the most obvious causes of why an electronic, mechanical, or other doodad might be misbehaving. It's usually something really unusual going on.

～

O n the last Trip in *Jacie Sails* — just before we evacuated ahead of Hurricane Irma — we had an issue.

The gadget in the cockpit that controls the autohelm wasn't working. In fact, it didn't seem to want to turn on.

(As an aside, I let the boat yard install it in a location where if you sit on the starboard side of the cockpit, you can control it accidentally with your right hip. It can be a lot of fun when that happens.)

Stranger yet, the wind indicator thingy on the bulkhead in front of me wouldn't power up. Those two gadgets usually power up even if the chartplotter is off — we don't even need to flip any of the switches at the control panel.

As Murphy would have it, the chartplotter died right about the same time as Hurricane Irma came through, so when I came down the next time, I had that too deal with that too — and that's about enough for this guy to process at one time.

That's when we discovered the arcane and unexpected culprit behind the dead instruments.

Well, by "we," I mean I enlisted Victor, aboard *Nereyda*, to help me figure out what the heck was going on. Victor has a lot more sailing miles than me, and he seems to get to the root of things a little quicker.

Diagnosis, Doctor?

First, Victor asked about the crazy assemblage of cables sprouting from my helm pedestal without anything attached to them.

"That's where the new chartplotter is gonna go," I told him. We looked over the various cables: power, network, transducer. (Which was supposed to fit the new plotter, and didn't.)

"Do you have the manuals for the previous plotter?" he asked.

"I think I can find it 'em my iPhone here."

And *mirabile dictu*, that's exactly what I did. I pulled up Evernote, looked in the "Boat" folder, and bam! Installation manual for the Raymarine A-, C-, and E-series, diabolically all crammed into one booklet. Smugly, I texted it to Victor.

"Mine's the E-series," I told him.

Victor proceeded to pore over the tiny screen while I made him another rum and coke.

"Have you checked the fuse?"

"There's a fuse for this?"

"Sure, it's right there next to the X10 unit."

Um...okay.

"Behind the sofa cushion down there where we were looking a minute ago."

Right...

"Does this look burnt out?" I asked Victor. (My eyesight ain't great.)

"Yep, this one's toast."

Who knew?

So we borrowed another fuse from Peter on *Duende* (of course I didn't have one), popped it in...and guess what happened?

You got it! Suddenly I had not only a couple of working displays, I could now even tell *Jacie Sails* to maintain course while I went forward to mess with the mainsail. Or take a leak, or something.

But Noooooooo....

Now you'd think this might teach me some kind of valuable lesson about not overlooking the most obvious culprits when trying to fix something.

But maybe I'm a little slow sometimes.

Not two days later, I was trying to fix another problem — the bilge sniffer alarm kept going off.

Normally having the alarm go off would be something I'd want to take careful notice of. But not so much in this case. Since the sensor had stopped working, I'd disconnected it.

(Not to worry, we hadn't had a working propane stove or any propane hooked up in a year.)

Anyway, the alarm at the nav desk was just going off seemingly at random, so I wanted to disconnect the power and shut the damn thing up. But — as I gather it should be for these alarm-type things — the power was permanently tied to the batteries and there was no switch on the control panel that would turn off the alarm, even if I flipped off the "DC MAIN" switch.

So I figured I'd just disconnect the power wire from the back of the alarm buzzer thingie.

(Easier said than done.)

I tried pulling gently on the alarm, which looked just like a little round faceplate, about two inches wide, mounted on the wall next to the nav desk.

I've found that a lot of these things are just held in place with little plastic flanges that only break about half of the time I mess with them...which occasions are apparently what they make caulk for.

But the thing didn't budge.

Okay, what about the high water alarm above it. Does it come out? I wondered.

Yes it did. But apparently the propane alarm was bolted in.

Okay, time for Part Two, I thought.

I unscrewed and pulled forward the panel next to the two alarms without damaging anything too much, and managed — barely — to get my hand in the hole, around the wires, and gingerly disconnect the connector I saw leading into the back of the alarm.

No go...other than I managed to set the alarm off a couple more times. Apparently those wires were from the sensor, not the power.

But I did see a red wire coming off a different part of the alarm.

That's gotta be the power...but where does that wire go?

The red wire went into a bundle with a bunch of other red wires and then up behind the main control panel. I had no idea where it ended up, but I was determined to find out.

It ran over towards...

...the fuse panel I had "discovered" a couple of days before.

And didn't I remember a label over one of the fuses that said "Alarm?" (Actually there were three. The guy at the boat yard must have been feeling creative, because they said "Fire Alarm," "Alarm System" and "High Water Alarm" — only one of which I actually have.)

So I pulled the fuse out that said "Alarm System." That did nothing.

Then I pulled the fuse that said "Fire Alarm."

WOO-HOO! The red light on the alarm unit went out, and peace returned to the ship.

A Slow Learner

Now you might think I'd have learned my lesson the first time with the fuses, and you might think I should now be learning not to over-look the obvious.

But I doubt that's gonna happen.

First of all, as I mentioned, I'm kinda slow sometimes. Secondly, what's obvious to you may not be obvious to me. As a multimedia ninja, I *use* computers and electronics a lot — but I don't dissect 'em for a living.

In the past, I'd often forget that electric things have fuses in them. But now that I've seen this handy trick in action a couple of times, hopefully I'll remember it.

But now I'll have to discover some other obvious thing to overlook.

I'm sure I won't have to wait too long.

PART II

HOW NOT TO HAVE FUN

A NEW ANCHORING TECHINIQUE

Boy, have I got a great new anchoring technique for you — especially if you don't mind breaking or losing a few fingers or damaging your boat. I call it "anchoring underway."

❧

I can pinpoint the exact date that I pioneered this exciting technique.

It was December 30th, 2013.

The Admiral and I were motoring in a disorganized sea from St. Pete to Cabbage Key for our first taste of their annual New Years Eve costume party. I'd already sailed solo to the Keys and back, and was anxious to demonstrate to Tanya what a competent sailor I'd become.

As we headed south from Pass-a-Grille towards Venice, the high temperature buzzer went off — a regular occurrence the first six months after bringing *Jacie Sails* from the lake to the ocean.

I killed the engine, and as we drifted on the greasy sea, I crammed the upper half of my body into the side of the engine compartment, upside down, and verified that the heat exchanger was leaking.

You can find a lot of drama anchoring if you do it right.

Topsides, after a bit of vomiting that felt like a giant had grabbed me around the waist and suddenly squeezed as hard as possible, I decided we'd need to call off the trip and return to port, since we'd never make it to Cabbage Key in time for New Years. But first, I placed a call to Captain David #2.

David informed me that the boat had originally been raw water cooled, and that I could simply bypass the heat exchanger and the second water pump, and run the engine "old school." Fewer parts to go wrong, but maybe a shorter engine life. That sounded like a fine bargain to me — at least for the time being — and we sailed into Egmont Channel to anchor behind Egmont Key so I could make the modification.

Maybe I was a little addled from the vomiting, from which I was still just recovering. At any rate, as we got to the inside (the east side) of Egmont Key and turned toward the beach, I gratefully threw the anchor off the bow. Still probably making two or three knots. Downwind.

The author, playing with the cooling system.

As the chain started to run out, I suddenly remembered a little tidbit that we learned in Sailboat 101: You're supposed to turn upwind before anchoring, and lower the hook when your momentum has slowed to approximately...zero. Oops.

At 3 knots, or three nautical miles per hour, that's 6076.12 feet per hour; or, with the anchor down, about 5 feet of chain running out over the bow each second.

Thank god I happened to be wearing gloves. Standing astride the anchor well in the bow, I tried to grab at the chain at moments when its wild rush slowed a little — but I couldn't stop it. And still we were headed toward the beach.

This is not going to be good, I thought. I've got to get a wrap of chain around the samson post or we're going to be seeing Egmont up close and personal. I tried to grab the chain again, and felt a couple of the fingers on my right glove rip. The chain was running out too fast to wrap it around the post without wrapping my fingers with it.

Finally, the momentum of our 18,000 pound vessel slowed just a little — not much, but just enough. Somehow, I managed to grab enough chain out of the locker to throw a loop around the samson post before that section of chain rushed over the bow roller. Immediately, our bow jerked around to port as the chain rode came taught, we spun in a half circle, and assumed the direction we should have been pointing to begin with.

I checked my hands: All of my fingers were still there, but my right glove was ripped to shreds. I sat down heavily on the bow and stayed there for a few minutes before I could think about working on the engine.

∾

So if you consider those kind of unnecessary and potentially dangerous maneuvers to be fun, then you can try anchoring that way some time.

As for me, I'm pretty sure that lesson will stick with me forever.

Since that day, I've made sure to anchor the right way: by turning upwind (or up-current, if the current is more of a factor) so I can carefully lower the anchor right where I want it, just as our momentum has slowed to nothing; and can easily pay out as much rode as we need while the boat begins to be float back downwind or down-current.

9

BAREFOOT AND CAREFREE

THERE'S NOTHING SO "SALTY" as strolling the decks barefooted: The sun on your feet, the salt water caressing your soles as your boat heels perfectly in a moderate breeze, and...

~

Ouch! What the hell was THAT? you say, as your foot sends an unmistakable "Screw you, pal!" to your brain.

Probably a cleat or something that you wouldn't have nearly broken your toe on if you were wearing deck shoes. The fact is, every boat has an ample number of things that protrude from the deck, cabin top, standing rigging...and of course, the aptly named toe rail.

And one of these protruding, non-moving objects will, without fail, find your unclad feet. Trust me.

I've actually heard of people breaking their toes on various of these protruding hazards. And that seems like a bad thing. Especially if you're out at sea by yourself.

And that sun kissing the tops of your tootsies? A little bit goes a long way. If your feet are anything like mine, they are the perfect angle (flat) and color (white) to catch every bit of that UV goodness. If I don't put on some sunscreen, they start to look like a pair of red snapper.

Of course, once you slather a couple of dollops of bargain sunscreen onto the tops of your feet, it will tend to sweat down to the bottom of your feet...which leads me to this:

There's an even more serious issue with going barefoot. As much as you'd like to think otherwise, your bare soles — even conditioned by months on the water — are just not as nonskid as the rubber soles on a pair of legit deck shoes. (As if to prove the point, I just walked outside in my bare feet here in Atlanta where it's been raining, and almost went ass over teakettle on the slippery garage floor.)

I consider it a good practice to stay aboard, particularly when sailing solo. Likewise, I think it wise to avoid falling and hitting my head — which is easy enough to do even under the most benign conditions with a gin and diet tonic in hand.

A trusty pair of deck shoes is the way to go when you're underway. Save the barefoot part for when you're at anchor.

But finding that perfect pair of deck shoes can be a challenge. The long-suffering pair that I'm wearing right now are a pair of white Sperry sneakers with navy and red trim. I liked the fit so much that I had the last pair shipped from a West Marine store in Alaska. I kid you not. The very last pair in my size of the Sperry "Spinnaker" model. I hope they bring them back.

This pair has a rip across the mesh atop the left big toe, and dabs of purple-brown epoxy filler.

This is my third pair of these babies. My second pair, due to a mistake, was actually one from my first pair and one from my second pair. (I accidentally threw out the wrong shoe.)

Now, you may be thinking, "Sneakers? That's not nautical at all." Well, that's not the worst of it, fella. I even wear socks with them.

But you know what? My feet have a pretty good grip on the deck when I'm out on the ocean by myself, and I don't have to worry about my bare, sweaty feet slipping inside the shoes, like I do with my leather docksiders. (Trust me, that can be dangerous, too.)

So do yourself a favor, and save the barefoot thing for when you're at anchor and do *not* have an adult beverage in hand.

10

DON'T BORE ME WITH RULES

WHO BUYS a boat to have to learn a bunch of new rules? I wanna escape the 9 to 5 world, not cater to The Man! Besides, none of the folks out in the ICW on weekends and holidays bothers with "the rules." So why should I?

~

Of course, the ICW attracts plenty of idiots — particularly on holidays during the high season. This is where the renters of rental boats, weekend warriors, and sons and daughters of legitimate boat owners ply their special brand of annoyance.

Very few of these people are sailing. They want to get where they're going as quickly, loudly, and drunkenly as possible. I'm all for the latter, of course; but show some respect, will ya?

Rules of the road? Forget it. Common sense? Ditto. (That's one reason I like to get out in the Gulf.)

But that doesn't let *you* off the hook.

Let me ask you this: How much did you pay — or are you planning to pay — for that new sailboat? Yeah...a lot. And you'd hate to be paying a salvage fella to haul it up off the bottom, right?

That's what I thought.

And if you don't know the rules of the road, that just might be your lot.

A lmost every time I go for a bike ride in my hilly Atlanta neighborhood, I'm reminded of one of the most important concepts about driving a boat, even though it's not a "rule," exactly.

> Make it clear to other boats what you are doing. If you're going to turn, *make it obvious.* If you're going to maintain your course, *make it obvious.* For bonus points, *be doing the right thing.*

This is what some of the well-meaning drivers in my neighborhood fail to understand. As sure as the sun rises, I'll be coming down a hill, hoping to keep a little momentum for the next climb...and the driver at the bottom of the hill *in front of me* will freeze like a startled squirrel.

They have plenty of time to make their turn and be on their way, but nope. They will inevitably sit at the stop sign while I grind to a screeching halt behind them. At which point they will slowly and painfully creep away from the stop sign and mosey on their way.

Sigh.

That's what some boaters will do. As they converge on another boat, they'll make a tiny, almost imperceptible course correction.

Are they turning to starboard? the other captain will wonder. *Or are they holding course?*

Of course, it also helps to actually know who's got the right of way and who needs to turn and stay the hell out of the way. When two sailboats converge, it can get tricky.

In general, a sailboat will have the right of way over a motor vessel unless it's fishing or barging, or mine-hunting, or what have you. So that container ship should theoretically give you the right of way.

But there's a really important *informal* rule we call "The Law Of Gross Tonnage." And it basically says that if you find yourself converging on a container ship or ocean liner or anything a lot bigger than you, it makes sense to give it a wide berth.

There's an old joke that shows even an aircraft carrier isn't immune from this rule:

Carrier Captain: Please divert your course 15 degrees to the north to avoid a collision.
Other Guy: Recommend you divert *your* course 15 degrees to the south to avoid a collision.
CC: This is the Captain of a US Navy ship. I say again, divert *your* course.
OG: No. I say again, you divert YOUR course.
CC: This is the aircraft carrier *USS Lincoln*, the second largest ship in the United States Atlantic fleet. We are accompanied by three destroyers, three cruisers and numerous support vessels. I demand that YOU change your course 15 degrees north — that's one-five degrees north — or countermeasures will be undertaken to ensure the safety of this ship.
OG: This is a lighthouse. Your call[1].

There's also a rule I just made up, called "The Law Of Idiots."

Give idiots a wide berth.

11

SPECIES OF ICW IDIOTS

Asshat In A Tall Ship

ONE DAY last Spring The Captain ran out of diesel. (I blame myself. I really do.)

No problem, The Captain explained to The Admiral and her niece and nephew. *After all, we're a sailboat.*

At Sarasota, we took a mooring ball under sail and spent the night, as The Captain tried unsuccessfully to clear a massive air lock in the engine. The next morning, we decided to head north under sail, back towards Gulfport.

We narrowly missed T-boning a very nice couple in the mooring field as we cast off under sail; but their prompt action averted disaster. As we pinched northward (almost directly into the wind) up the ICW towards Tampa Bay, I spied a southbound power boat.

Well, not really a power boat. More like a fast moving building. It was three stories tall and I could see the bow wave from a mile away.

It blew by our group of three sailboats without slowing down in the slightest, leaving us to thrash about in its vast wake. Needless to say, it completely obliterated the tiny bit of momentum we had under sail. (Not that the the idiot at the helm would have known or cared that we were not under power.)

I could see no glimpse of the "Captain" through the tinted windows high above, but I could picture him. An asshole wearing CHiPs mirrored shades and one of those white captain's hats.

As he passed us, I grabbed the air horn and gave him five quick blasts along with a middle finger. By that time he was already astern of us by the length of a football field. We could follow his progress southward by the VHF radio traffic. Cursing is prohibited, but you can read between the lines sometimes:

"Thanks for the slow pass."

"This is a no wake zone, Cap'n."

I hope the local authorities caught him, but that's probably too optimistic.

Don't be that guy. If you're out in the Gulf, it's one thing. Open 'er up and let the blowboats do what they gotta. (Presumably, you're not within fifty feet of them, and hopefully they have a breeze to maneuver.) But if you're in a constricted area, have a clue what's going on around you. Just sayin'...

Young, Dumb, and full of…beer.

And here is another type. Kids (I say "kids"now) with Daddy's boat. Or a rental…a lotta places aren't too picky these days.

Now don't get me wrong. There are young people who have grown up on the water and know what they're doing. And then there are…these.

Their music is your music. If you're in a sailboat, then you must be an Old Fart. As with most other powerboaters, they have no clue whether you're traveling under power or under the fickle caress of the wind.

Not long ago, one such group blew by me while I was becalmed in the narrow channel next to Jewfish Key. When I shouted and gestured for them to slow down, they yelled back something about them not realizing there was a speed limit here.

Of course there isn't. But there is a no wake rule. Or perhaps it's just a guideline. (Okay, it's only a rule under bridges and near marinas and stuff. I just checked.)

At any rate, there is definitely a tradition, upheld by almost nobody, to slow down and reduce one's wake when passing a vessel under sail in a constricted area. And it is a U.S. (and international) rule that powerboats must give way to sailboats. Unless specific other rules apply. You can see where this might get a little too complicated for the average teen with a few Budweisers in him.

Still, given that said drunken teens are not likely towing a barge or engaged in commercial fishing, the basic rule of thumb is this:

A sailboat is dependent on the wind and floats much closer to the bottom than your pontoon boat or runabout. Kindly slow your ass down and don't force them into grounding on the side of the channel.

The Considerate Dope

One notable species is the Considerate Dope. He (let's face it, 90 percent of the people I see at the helm — and close to 100 percent of the worst offenders — are male) thinks he is doing you a favor by slowing down. 75 feet from you. Apparently not realizing that the wake of his huge sport fisher or cabin cruiser actually travels, and does not stop when he does.

As a matter of fact, I believe the wake tends to get *bigger* when a big boat suddenly slows down.

Oh, well. At least they're trying. And there's a lot to be said for at least *considering* the other boaters around you and making an effort to learn the rules of the road.

12

MORE FUN WITH ANCHORS

THE 192 MILE nonstop solo leg started out well enough. Twenty-four hours earlier, I cast off at 3:38 in the morning and motored out of Pass-a-Grille below St. Pete Beach into the Gulf of Mexico. The occasional "washing machine" effect in the pass there was thankfully absent, and I headed due south across the Tampa Bay shipping channel and past Egmont Key.

Not long after dawn, a noisy but somehow familiar racket clattered up forward. After a precious few seconds my brain made the connection, and I leapt forward and acted just in time to keep the anchor and its entire rode from going overboard. The bitter end was actually not secured to anything, so that would have been it for my main anchor — it would have sunk without a trace.

So there I was, with my 35 pound anchor, 200 pounds of chain, and most of the rope rode out, in thirty feet of water. The wind, while not fresh, was nonetheless starting to push against my nine-ton vessel enough to make hauling her by hand back up to the anchor even more difficult. Also, we have no windlass of any kind. It's all manpower in the literal sense.

Ninety minutes of pure hell later, I finally heaved the anchor out of the water and secured it in the bow roller, and lashed it — with much more care this time — to the bitt.

PART III

HOW NOT TO BE SAFE

13

DOCKING MADE SIMPLE

*Docking a sailboat is easy anyway...but **follow these simple rules, and I guarantee everyone on the dock will be applauding you.***

~

D ocking a nine-ton cruising sailboat is *not* simple, and if there is anyone on the dock, they will be laughing at you. Your rare flawless docking or undocking will occur when there is absolutely nobody around to witness it.

"Not me. I was a master at maneuvering the family runabout!" you may protest.

Maybe so, Grasshopper. But there are some unique and challenging things about a cruising sailboat, and one of them is...

Prop walk.

Prop walk has to do with the centrifugal motion of the flux capacitor, or something like that. But what it boils down to is this: When you put your sailboat in forward gear and turn the wheel (or tiller), the boat generally goes in the direction you want.

When you put a sailboat in reverse and give it some juice, the ass end immediately pulls to one side (usually the left), no matter which way you're trying to steer. Even if you think you're all set to motor straight backwards. If you're backing into or out of a slip (you're going to have to do one or the other), this means your stern is going to want to clonk right into the dock.

The good news is, you can eventually learn to use this evil magic to your advantage. You can back out and do a "270" to the right, alternating bursts of forward and reverse, instead of just backing out and turning left like you wanted to. After a number of times doing this in a narrow marina channel, you may not even need to change your shorts.

When you're docking on a seawall, if you can manage to get the bow tied to something on land, you can then put 'er in reverse, and use the prop walk to pull the stern gently toward the cleat, even if the wind or current wants to pull you away from the dock. (Up to a point.)

Oh, yeah. Wind and current. They are your enemies now. That perfect docking you make in a flat calm, which fills you with pride in your amazing seamanship and may even tempt you to buy a cap with an anchor and the word "Captain" embroidered on it, becomes an absolute circus when you throw in a strong breeze. Or even a moderate breeze, in your case.

The above-the-water part of your sailboat, which I understand is called the topsides, will catch the wind. More than you think. The wind will push on your hull above the water, the cabin top, and the mast and boom, even without sails up. And since the front part of the boat is usually a little higher than the back, and therefore more affected by the wind, the wind will push the bow of your boat toward the pristine yacht in the next slip downwind.

You were certain you could get your nose in the slip at least, but that isn't even happening. You have to bail out and go around again — but you don't have enough space to do it. You're about to ram the pointy part of your heavy boat into their freshly painted "Nauti Nights," or whatever it says on their transom.

So you jam it into reverse at full throttle without bothering to visit neutral (not recommended)...and find that your ass end is now headed toward another boat.

You yell at your mate to fend off — and then tell her not to, since there's no way even a russian powerlifter on steroids could counteract the forces involved. Maybe you manage to hold a fender between your boat and theirs, jam it back into forward at full throttle, and manage to get off with only pulling their dinghy and bending their dinghy davits just the *tiniest* bit. Not that that's ever happened to me.

Everyone will have come sprinting down the dock to offer help, get a firsthand look, shake their heads and mutter amongst themselves, and make sure you don't crash into their boat. But maybe not in that order.

If you're luckier, the wind may be from the stern. If you can get the nose in, your only challenge will be not crashing into the dock locker. You'll get the nose in and throw it into reverse as you realize you're coming in way too hot...and your stern will promptly jump sharply to port, banging into the dock on that side.

With gratitude, you'll hand the wrong lines to a nervous-looking dockmate or two, who will offer two completely different versions of how you should have done it — the subtext of which will be how your way was obviously, totally, wrong and lubberly.

Then you'll vow never to take the boat out again.

(Not really. Because you love being out on the water in your own boat, because you still don't know what you don't know, and because God does indeed appear to love the Stupid.)

No, you'll take the boat out again the next time the exact same conditions obtain, secure in the knowledge that you've already failed in this exact drill, and that you know how to solve it.

Except that, as you approach your slip this time, under the *exact* same wind, the boat is doing something new and different.

Okay. So the wind is astern. Okay, so it's going to want to blow us straight into the dock box, but I should be able to get the nose in. Wait... what the @#(*&@#$#?!?? Why am I headed for Nauti Nights *again? Oh, shit!*

"GRAB A FENDER!"

Don't feel bad. It was the current this time. Everything *is* exactly the some up above the water, but this week, the tide has changed, and the current is pushing the five feet or so of hull under the boat straight for *Nauti Nights*.

Did I mention you should always, *always* have a bailout plan? By "bailout plan," I don't mean a plan to abandon ship. (Although that's good, too.) I mean a plan to go around safely and try again if your plan doesn't pan out like you thought, without running into expensive things like other boats, or people or concrete or rocks.

If you're lucky, the bailout plan will work. If not, well...join the club. They say there are only two kinds of sailors: those who have run aground, and liars. This applies to "docking fails" as well.

> Now, in all seriousness, my attorney wishes for me to say that you should not take docking (or running into *Nauti Nights*, or *Moonbeam*, or *Windbreaker*) lightly. And that's true. A nine-ton boat can do a lot of damage, even at one knot. It can damage your wallet, it can damage your fingers, hands, feet, toes, legs, and other body parts, and it can damage your pride. Your pride will recover, but the other things may not.

So maybe you should (gasp) actually *practice* docking, somewhere other than at the dock. Somewhere you won't run into expensive things, or people or concrete or rocks. Maybe a mooring ball far away from other boats can serve as a stand-in for your slip. (Note: the authorities tend to frown upon tying up to navigation markers and signs and buoys and whatnot. Doing so could also damage your wallet and your pride.)

Once you start getting the hang of what your boat will do in different winds and currents, you should be able to get into and out of your slip in style. Most of the time. Then you can be one of those folks sprinting down the dock to try and prevent some idiot from running into *your* boat.

Oh. And doesn't leaving the marina to practice on a mooring ball or something necessarily involve docking and undocking?

Why, yes. Yes, it does.

14

LIGHTNING IS OVERRATED

WHY WORRY ABOUT LIGHTNING? After all, you've got a fifty foot lightning rod sticking up out of the boat. And besides, the odds are tiny that your boat (or you) will ever be struck.

~

I'll be honest. My relationship with lightning on the water has never been casual. It's had its ups and downs.

Just a few weeks after The Admiral and I christened *Jacie Sails* off St. Pete, I started south on a solo trip to the Keys, via Cabbage Key. We'd barely wet our feet in the Gulf, but I've always been fairly determined about pressing forward.

(There's a fine line between "determined" and "stupid," but we'll leave that for another spot.)

As I cleared Pass-a-Grille Point and turned left past Egmont Key, one of the typical late-August "dailies" (daily summer thunderstorms) that had been churning up over the land began to spill out over the Gulf.

A photo I shot at the time shows a beautiful multicolored canopy of high clouds as I look westward. But behind me as I shot the picture was a nasty-looking thunderstorm, of which those beautiful clouds were just the advance team.

Soon, the water was getting choppy. Nothing to write home about, as I was to learn — but on my first solo trip in salt water, I was nervous. I pulled the mainsail down into the lazy jacks and cranked up the engine, as lightning licked Bradenton, Longboat Key and Sarasota to my west every ten seconds or so.

Due to the statute of limitations, I can only say that earlier I may or may not have lit my first and last joint ever as a captain. And if so, I believe part of my thinking would have been to prevent nausea. Instead, I got just a hint of paranoia. Between the choppy water, stress and moderate exercise of messing with the sails, I was feeling queasy, despite any "medication" I may or may not have been taking.

I steered SSW until I was about twelve miles off Siesta Key, and things settled down a bit. I made overnight for Boca Grande Channel, where I'd jump back into the ICW to reach Cabbage Key.

Okay, I thought, I can work with this. Just keep the zillion-volt light show as far away as possible.

At daybreak, I headed into Boca Grande and things were good. Once inside, I turned south a few miles to Cabbage Key, and spent a day or two getting to know the place and the cool folks there. Then, after an early breakfast with Rob Wells, the owner of Cabbage Key, it was back out Boca Grande and south toward Marathon.

As night fell, I was parallel with Marco Island, watching the thunderstorms build over the Everglades and also pop up in the Gulf around me. I kept an eye on the lightning and the clouds it illuminated, and turned on the radar sparingly, to save power.

At one point during the night, a thunderstorm managed to sneak up behind me. You'd think this would be hard to do, but I managed to miss it until it was maybe five to seven miles behind me.

(Sounds like a decent margin, but it doesn't feel that way at sea at night — and lightning can strike several miles from the cloud it comes from.)

I altered course to avoid the main couple of storms that bedeviled me, and ended up sailing east and west, toward and then away from the Everglades.

Finally, I was able to head south again, and with dawn came one of my most memorable moments so far.

At first light I was motoring south in the middle of Florida Bay on water like glass. Cumulus and Cumulonimbus clouds, pink in the sunrise, dotted the horizon from the Everglades to Key West.

I hung on to the starboard shrouds to take a leak.

Ahhhhhhhh. Now this is just amazing.

Nothing around but me, *Jacie Sails*, and the water. And fish and turtles and dolphin. (And lobster pots. Can't have it all, I guess.)

I made it down to Seven Mile Bridge by late afternoon and anchored next to Knights Key Bank, after dodging another thunderstorm and a waterspout and sailing south past East Bahia Honda Key and a zillion lobster pot buoys.

Unfortunately, I had to spend Labor Day weekend "stuck" in Marathon until I could find a machinist to fix my water pump pulley. Every so often ya have to take one for the team.

But my takeaway from my first trip south during the summer was: Respect the lightning, but don't freak out about it.

Famous last words.

∿

Since my trip in 2013 was such a brilliant success, I decided to take The Admiral to Marathon in 2015, again in late August. I explained to her that we might have to dodge some thunderstorms, but that they were manageable and we'd be prudent about it. I hadn't killed her yet, so she trusted me on this.

Everything went as advertised as we headed south to Sanibel. There were some of the usual dailies kicking up over land, but nothing to worry us. We had a nice overnight sail and enjoyed the heck out of Sanibel.

At Sanibel, though, we got our first real light show of the cruise. In the evening, a powerful storm built up over Ft. Myers and stretched out toward us, with ground strikes as near as the Sanibel Causeway. It was loud and close.

Still, we took off the next day — my birthday — south out into the Gulf from San Carlos Bay.

Maybe I should have taken it as an omen when we got boarded by the Coast Guard. But we passed inspection, and I told The Admiral she could hand me back the beer I hadn't officially been drinking when the Coasties pulled up.

After spending an unplanned stop that night in Naples to repair the cutlass bearing that had just been "repaired" a week earlier, we headed south again, only to be driven back by a thunderstorm near Marco Island. I damn near ran Jacie up onto the beach to get as close to the high rise condos as possible, and anchored. I wanted to make sure there was something else taller nearby.

So for two days we'd been stymied: once by the cutlass bearing and once by lightning. The next morning we set out south again from Marco, determined to make Marathon.

We sailed south along the coast, passing Cape Romano, and by afternoon the Everglades were about twelve miles to port.

I remember, as Tanya napped, seeing a line of small thunderstorms some miles off our starboard bow, and one thunderstorm off the port bow. They seemed to be almost stationary. I decided to try to squeeze between them.

But the closer I got to the gap, the more the two systems seemed to converge. It was like some kind of Harry Potter movie where a huge diabolical stone gate is about to slam shut on Our Hero. I didn't see a lot of lightning in these systems, but I didn't want to be underneath them.

Thankfully, we managed to squirt through the gap. I only spied one more storm far off our starboard bow, and I figured we'd be able to scoot past that one.

And that was the one that kicked our asses.

No, I don't have any pictures of it — for a couple of very good reasons. One reason is that we had bigger fish to fry, as it were. Another is that our house batteries seemed to be running down, and the chartplotter was acting wacky. All we had left was our i-Gadgets and a handheld GPS that unfortunately didn't have any useful charts loaded on it. We turned off the autohelm to conserve power and cranked up the engine to try and charge the batteries.

This storm seemed to just keep growing, and it absolutely hammered us all evening and night. No big wind or waves. Just thunder and lightning.

At one point, Tanya was sitting athwartships on the cockpit floor between the port and starboard benches, holding a square boat cushion over her head. I wasn't sure it would do much to prevent electrocution, but I didn't want to burst her bubble.

After a while, she retreated (wisely) belowdecks, and I advised her to stay away from the mast...and, well, any electrical stuff. After all, we were the only thing for a dozen miles in any direction that wasn't flat. In fact, we had this big metal pole sticking up into the air like a ridiculously easy target. Tickling the bottom of the clouds and shouting, "We're here!"

And then came a thunderclap like no other. It was simultaneous with a lighting strike that momentarily blinded me. It couldn't have been more than fifteen hundred feet away, and it felt like it was right there in the cockpit.

I leapt through the companionway into the cabin and away from the metal wheel I'd been holding for hours. I didn't give a damn which way the boat was going. I was going to make absolutely sure the same deadly blast wasn't about to repeat.

After a minute or so, I very gingerly crawled out into the cockpit, flicked on the autohelm, pointed us south again, and scurried back to the cabin for a few minutes. The autohelm might run out our batteries, but so be it.

As it turns out, the autohelm did pretty much finish off the batteries...and with them, any ability to use the chartplotter...or charge our i-Gadgets. So we limped into Marathon using my paper charts of the Keys (See "Who Needs Paper Charts?") and the little handheld GPS with no charts on it — just latitude and longitude numbers.

We didn't have any more strikes like the one that made our hair stand on end, but that doesn't mean conditions were awesome. By the time we got to Marathon, we decided that The Captain had been far too sanguine about the late summer dailies in South Florida — and that we might be making different plans in the future.

~

So while I still don't "freak out" about lightning, I'm at that stage in our relationship where I give it a wide berth.

I don't want to jinx anything here (not that I'm superstitious at all), but between wind, waves, and lightning: Lightning bothers me the most — at least in my cruising area. I feel like you can avoid systems with high wind and waves by staying in port — and I plan to continue to do just that! — but those daily thunderstorms brewing all summer in South Florida are the real deal.

15

MARKERS ARE FOR WIMPS

Like, DUH. We have an app for that now. Other than making sure you don't run over one, those channel markers and other thingies out there are pretty much just for historical interest.

I'm sure you've heard the old saying: There are only two kinds of sailors: Those who've run aground...and liars.

So while you can be almost certain you'll go aground at some point, it's much more fun to do it less often.

The first time The Admiral and I headed south from Venice (Florida, not Italy) in the ICW, I ran aground more than once. Fortunately we didn't get stuck in the muddy bottom; but I tried out some new strings of curse words, and Tanya began to wonder if I knew what I was doing.

Part of my confusion stemmed from this: There were often no less than *three* opinions about where the safe part of the channel was!

First, there were the little icons of the channel markers on my chartplotter.

Then there was the little purple line on the chartplotter that showed (I think) where the Army Corps Of Engineers had determined the center of the channel was. Sometimes it was drawn completely outside the markers on the same chart.

What the...?!??

Finally, right there in real life, were the actual red and green signposts on big poles, sticking up out of the water.

How quaint.

Now, don't get me wrong. I'm not saying the actual markers are always right, either. I've run aground at least a hundred feet inside Marker 7 in the North Channel at Pass-a-Grille.

I've also learned that some of the huge metal floating marker buoys aren't even lit at night. (I almost clobbered one coming into Boca Grande my first time at night.)

But still, people do actually install the darned things after actually surveying the depth and checking reports of problem areas. And they're not prone to bad satellite or cellular coverage, or any of that mess.

So I'd say ya might just want to keep an eye on 'em.

16

WHO NEEDS PAPER CHARTS?

WHO WANTS to carry around a bunch of paper charts? I have a chart-plotter in front of me, an iPhone and an iPad. What could possibly go wrong?

〜

W ell, a lot, actually. And don't think it won't happen to you! Paper charts can come in *really* handy, even if you're not going all old-school with a compass.

I was reminded of this when we got our asses kicked (and the house batteries went Tango Uniform) on our way from Marco Island to Marathon in August 2015.

As I mentioned in "Lightning Is Overrated," we had been hammered all afternoon, evening and night by thunderstorms, and the chartplotter went on strike when the house voltage went below 11.5 volts. Then the iPad died, with my Navionics chart on it. Then the iPhone, with same. Then Tanya's iPhone.

At three in the morning or so, we'd had enough for a while, and dropped the hook a few miles north of Marathon. But around dawn, we thought we'd make a break for shelter.

The problem was, we had no navigational gadgets. What I *did* have was a seven-year-old Garmin GPS, which could tell us where on the face of the Earth we were...but had no charts of the area loaded, for some reason.

Zero. Zilch. Nada. Just an arrow on the LCD screen showing where we were and which way we'd be headed once we got underway, and the ability to enter a destination waypoint — at which point it would give us a line to follow.

So there I am, an overweight bearded man in his underwear, in a hail storm, asking The Admiral to try to hold the big paper chart book so it wouldn't blow away (there's a pretty funny video on YouTube if you're not put off by overweight bearded men in underwear), and trying to find latitude and longitude numbers from the edges of the pages in order to enter a waypoint into my handheld battery-powered GPS.

I started with where we were on the GPS, and got the coordinates. Then I looked at where that was on the paper chart. Then I'd find the next place we could travel to on the chart without running aground. And I'd consult the edges of the paper chart to see what the coordinates were for *that*. And I'd enter those into the GPS to give us a path through the coral.

It was a long morning.

But if we hadn't had the nice spiral-bound book of large paper charts for Florida, we'd have been extra screwed.

I don't know what we would have done. But let's just say that as we played haul-up-the-anchor to get underway, we saw the Coasties helping a guy off his boat just a couple miles away.

We heard later that the Coasties had rescued a captain and his pit bull off a boat right in that area.

I bet he didn't have any paper charts.

17

WE'RE ONLY GOING IN THE DINGHY

*WE'RE ONLY GOING **in the dinghy. What could possibly go wrong?***

Tanya and I spent much of the day at West Marine, pursuing a new hobby we call "spending copious amounts of money." (Also known as "owning a boat.")

We bought about 220 feet of good quality rope for dock lines. (It's never "rope" after it assumes its new nautical purpose; it must be referred to as a "line," or you may be taunted mercilessly.)

We also bought 85 feet of 3/8" BBB anchor chain (which is quite heavy), and a 35 pound Delta anchor.

We had three Danforth anchors from Lake Lanier, but only one was suitable for "salty" use. The other two were undersized and one of those was rusty and bent.

The Delta is good for holding in sandy bottoms and anchorages where the Danforth anchor may not be as effective. So now we should have two good alternatives, which can also be deployed in tandem if need be.

After all that money-spending, we headed back to Jacie Sails and worked for a while stashing these new items, and re-stashing some of the old ones. We eventually worked up a fair hunger and thirst.

Tanya and I discussed driving somewhere (like The Chattaway, one of our "off campus" favorites), and the possibility of actually taking the dinghy over to Gulfport, a mile or two by water. It was getting close to sundown, but we had yet to even try lowering the "dink" from the davits on the stern where it had hung since it was delivered to Salt Creek during Jacie Sails' refit.

After dithering a few minutes, something clicked. Or perhaps snapped.

"Screw it, let's go," I said. (Or something similar.) You only live once, right? I threw the red five gallon gas tank into the dink, jerked the lines holding her out of their cam cleats, and lowered away until she floated on the calm marina water just astern of the boat.

Tanya and I did the limbo under the solar panel, climbed down the stern ladder, and hopped into our "new used" dinghy. The outboard motor fired right up in a most gratifying manner, and we tooled out of the marina like two very proud parents. Off to a new adventure in the gathering night.

Without life jackets. Or a light for the dinghy. Or an "audio signaling device." Oops. (Fear not! I have since made a habit of including these things...)

Now, in fairness, we planned to hug the shore of Boca Ciega Bay, in water pretty much too shallow for sailboats or really anything other than kayaks or rafts.

Therein lies the rub. Halfway between the marina and the Gulfport waterfront district, the outboard started sputtering.

Uh oh, I thought. I bet we've snagged a lobster buoy or some kind of line in this shallow water. *Or maybe there's water in the fuel line. Or something...*

I put the outboard in neutral and pulled the lanyard to kill the motor, just in case. Then I reached down into the dark water towards the propeller and found...

Mud.

One might assume that with our tiny draft, we could stay a couple of hundred yards from shore and be fine.

But one would be wrong if one were to assume such a thing. We hadn't snagged something in the prop. We had run aground. The prop was trying to claw its way through the sand and silt that lined the bottom of this part of the bay. Good thing it wasn't rock, or coral, or a herd of slumbering manatee or something.

After discovering my error, I had to grab the oars and row us out of the shallows before we could entertain the idea of using the outboard motor again. Tanya was — how shall we say? — laughing her ass off.

We were so shallow that for the first fifty yards or so, I was actually using the oars not to row, but to lever us forward by digging them into the muddy bottom just a few inches below us. (It was probably at this point that I cracked one of the plastic oarlocks, since repaired with duct tape.)

Finally, we escaped the shallows and were able to motor again towards dinner — and Tanya was finally able to breathe again.

I'm pleased to report we successfully made our way over to the Gulfport Casino dinghy dock, tied up and exited the dinghy without major embarrassment, grabbed some well-deserved food and drink at O'Maddy's overlooking the bay, and headed back to Jacie Sails without incident...this time keeping a much healthier distance from the invisible underwater point.

18

IT'S ONLY WEATHER.

Why worry about the weather? There's gonna be some anyway. After all, I have a schedule to keep. I gotta meet people. Then I have to get back to work.

S o on the crossing south to Cuba (with The Admiral), the sea was almost like glass. Of course. But on the way back north (solo)...

Not so much.

The fact is, the Gulf Stream can be ugly, especially where it runs west to east against the trade winds; so I suspect our smooth trip south was more of an exception than the rule. Pick your poison: winds in the winter, or lightning in the summer. Maybe we need to do it again in the spring or fall. I enjoyed Cuba anyway.

I haven't been in any "survival" storms so far — and I'd like to keep it that way — but I have been in some conditions that made me queasy.

On the way back across the Straits of Florida from Cuba I had to move from position to position in the cockpit to keep from hurling.

Aft upwind corner of the cockpit. (My left foot would get sore from standing at an angle.) Downwind side of the cockpit, near the companionway, looking up at the oncoming waves. (Nausea after a couple of minutes.) I went below as rarely and as quickly as possible.

Bob and Will aboard s/v *Walkabout* told me we had a favorable weather window for crossing back north, according to that weather guru guy. Since it was the last day for me to leave Cuba before I'd need some kind of special import license from some U.S. government entity, I went for it. *Walkabout* would presumably be somewhere in the vicinity during the crossing, anyway.

As I cleared the breakwater around 3 p.m., it was a little choppy. Not nearly the full-on Norther we'd had for the last few days, but choppy.

I angled ENE, looking like I was heading away, planning to curve back south toward Havana Harbor to get some shots of the Malecon and the fort. But between my distrust of the weather and of the strangely empty El Viejo y El Mar "hotel" overlooking my route, I gave that plan up and headed toward Sand Key Light. No telling what the invisible eyes in El Viejo y El Mar would think of my super telephoto lens.

As usual, the camera (especially facing downwind where the waves have been weakened by the boat) failed to convey the conditions — but they were not that bad compared to what was coming.

I spoke with *Walkabout* on the radio about three times. I remember speaking with Will, the "crew." Later in the night (or early in the morning) I spoke with Captain Bob. Apparently Will had gotten seasick and incapacitated. Bad news for Will, but I felt a little better about feeling like crap. I didn't toss my cookies, but like Bob, I wasn't far from it.

It's a fourteen hour passage from Marina Hemingway to Key West, and by the middle of the night I was toast. Nauseated, sore, and cranky. I had my Spot transmitter clipped to my Mustang survival vest, along with a laser beacon just in case I went over or something. I wasn't clipped in — which I am *not* recommending — but had zero intention of venturing forward from the cockpit.

As we neared the northern edge of the Gulf Stream — around the time I expected us to be out of the junk — the seas were ten feet and on the beam. I was not a happy camper. I know ten feet is nothing to write home about, but for me they were large. When I sat on the leeward bench, I'd look up at them. They would block the moon as they approached, just huge black chunks of water; but they passed under *Jacie* without breaking.

Like my first solo trip to the Dry Tortugas, I was beginning to wonder if I'd start vomiting; and if so, if I'd be able to manage the boat. Finally, around dawn, I made it into Key West Main Channel, dodged some vessels, including some triple-decker mini cruise ship thingie, and called the Coast Guard and Galleon Marina on the radio. I've rarely been so glad to see a marina as I was to see the Galleon that morning.

My point is this: Going out in marginal conditions, especially on an overnight passage, is no fun. Although I reckoned that I "had no choice" but to leave Cuba before my U.S. Customs permission ran out, I probably could have stayed if I needed to stay for safety reasons.

I want to strike a balance here. I feel like some cruisers stay in port for way too long, preparing to the *n*th degree, and waiting for the perfect weather window.

However, my attorney has advised me to say that you can't be too careful with the weather.

As for me, I'd hate to see you petrified with fear of going out with a less than ideal forecast. But if you don't love vomiting copiously and being scared, do yourself a favor and *do* take the weather into account!

PART IV

WHAT NOT TO DO

19

ALWAYS TRUST THE BOATYARD

Lifting the mast off the tractor trailer in St. Pete. That sucker is heavy.

EVERYONE *at the boatyard is a certified professional, so you've nothing to worry about. Even if you don't know exactly what you want, they will pick the best option for your boat and circumstance.*

Okay, so maybe not. Look, there are a lot of decent boatyards out there.

Well, at least a few. Okay, so maybe finding a decent boatyard or marine mechanic is like finding an honest man in a used car dealership.

The fact is, in my experience boatyards are busy places that place a premium on doing as much work on as many boats as quickly as possible. No faulting them on that, I suppose.

Some (okay, maybe a few) actually try to build a reputation as straight-up businesses. Good on 'em! But even those are hamstrung by a couple of challenges.

One is trying to find competent, dependable people among the salty community. Not saying my fellow boaters are "interesting," prone to drinking, and like to do their own thing. I wouldn't say that at all.

Another thing is that even if a boatyard is trying their best, *they can't read your mind*.

A good boatyard — and even a lot of the crappy ones — work on a lot of boats. If you don't know, or don't specify, exactly how you want things done, you probably won't get it done right.

For example, when I brought my boat down to St. Pete, I wanted a solar panel added, and I thought that on top of the dinghy davits was a reasonable place to put one.

Fair enough, but since I didn't say much else, nobody bothered to mention that (a) the solar panels would be at an angle, which wouldn't maximize the sun's rays; and (b) The Admiral and I would have to do the limbo under the panels every time we wanted to climb down into the dinghy. (The panels were also fixed in place, so we couldn't adjust the angle or anything.)

So after putting up with that for a while, I had to get Captain David #2 to install an extension above the davits to raise the solar panel. So now we can get into the dinghy with less fuss, and the panel gets a better charge all day. (Unfortunately, I'm not thrilled with what it does to the beautiful lines of the boat, but it does add some shade to the cockpit.)

Another example: Somebody (I don't know if it was the main yard or the rigging company) asked me if I wanted to keep the deck-level running lights, since I was installing masthead tricolor running lights.

"I guess not," I said. And so they cut the wires to the deck-level lights from the breaker panel.

Unfortunately, it turns out that for some arcane legal reasons — and so ships and things can tell what you are — you're supposed to have the deck level running lights on if you're motoring at night. (In addition to the steaming light halfway up the mast.) Oops.

And then there are the batteries. As I recall, *Jacie Sails* had one battery when we got her. It may have even been a golf cart battery or something like that.

When I moved the boat down to the ocean, I wanted to make sure everything was up to snuff for a cruising sailboat. Among the planned upgrades was installing a hefty bank of house batteries along with a separate cranking battery.

The lucky guy at the boatyard who got this task suggested I let him bolt a fiberglass shelf in the starboard cockpit locker to put the house batteries on.

"I guess so," I said. Unfortunately, now the only way I can access the cranking battery to do anything with it (like replace it, which I just did recently) is to jam myself into the port quarterberth, support myself with one arm over the prop shaft and perform the Prone Battery Lift™ with my other hand, which means I get to hoist a 56-pound battery through a small opening in the opposite side of the engine compartment, over the engine, and out through the quarterberth.

My friend Captain Mitch had suggested letting me deputize him to oversee the refitting process in St. Pete. Mitch has a lot of experience in exactly these matters, but I thought it might piss off the yard to have some "foreigner" looking over their shoulder. But perhaps Mitch had a point.

Then there are the times when a boatyard is just plain sloppy. I had a cutlass bearing that came out a couple of years ago, so I had *Jacie* towed to a boatyard in Gulfport which shall remain nameless.

If you don't know, we'll just say the cutlass bearing is the thingie that holds your prop shaft in place, and when it's out of place you don't want to be motoring.

Usually replacing the cutlass bearing is something you want to do with the boat out of the water; so I paid for the yard to haul her out and paid for a room at the Bilmar overnight, since the yard wasn't keen on letting me stay aboard on the hard.

I wanted to be sure we got the bearing fixed right, since The Admiral and I were cruising down to the Keys immediately. In fact, she arrived just as the yard was splashing the boat again. Of course, they left strap marks on *Jacie* from the re-launch, so I convinced the manager to do a quick scrub job on those.

Tanya and I were ready to go — or so we thought.

I think Ray Charles could have seen what was coming. We got as far south as Naples before the damned cutlass bearing came out again. (What's that, a whopping 150 miles?) After a few choice words, I got a refund on the cutlass bearing "repair," but of course no refund for the hotel stay.

Fortunately, we found a guy in Naples who came out and fixed the bearing — underwater, no less! — and that fix lasted over 2,000 miles, including trips to the Florida Keys, Dry Tortugas, and Cuba.

So I guess the good news is, you'll occasionally find good people when you need it most and expect it least. (Calypso Canvas and Sail in Key Largo comes to mind. Two thumbs up!) But the rest of the time, be ready to grit your teeth and grab your ankles.

At least the more you get to know your boat and the more you start to work on her yourself, the better a feel you'll develop for what to look for (and look out for) when dealing with boatyards and mechanics. In the meantime, it can be an expensive and frustrating process.

But you knew that, right?

My recommendation for new skippers is this: When it comes to boatyards, you probably want to have a long chat with somebody that knows their business, listen to them carefully, think about and weigh carefully what they tell you, ask them some *more* questions...and then try to be as specific as possible with the boatyard. And keep a sharp eye on what they're doing.

20

BLOCKHEADS (ALWAYS TRUST THE BOAT YARD?)

A HASTY REFIT. **What could possibly go wrong?**

∿

S o we had *Jacie Sails* in her new home, but one important thing remained. We still needed to do an official christening.

Saturday, June 29, 2013 we decided it was time to get on with it, and we were chomping at the bit. At the very least, we were going to take *Jacie Sails* for a spin in the bay — and perhaps even into the Gulf.

We managed to get from our slip to the fuel dock, using our prop walk in reverse to manage a decent landing, thanks to the patience of Our Man Tony.

We also managed to top off the diesel tank, and Tony gave us some advice on how to tell by listening that the tank is almost full — the particulars of which I promptly forgot once we left the dock.

As we left the dock, Tony was discreetly gesturing and calmly saying that we could bear more to starboard to avoid clobbering the end of the dock, and various boats beyond it. But we couldn't! *Jacie Sails* didn't seem to want to go to the right very much.

This probably should have set off a number of alarm bells, but I was already pretty much on overload with all these new things: docking and undocking at a fuel dock, fueling up and making sure we didn't spill fuel into the water, and guiding *Jacie Sails* out of this particular marina under power.

So, yeah, I wasn't 100% attuned to the whole "won't go to the right very much" issue. I (somehow) didn't notice anything amiss as we negotiated the 90 degree turn to starboard through the marina entrance channel past the most expensive boats in the place. From there it was a straight shot into the bay, and we were out!

Soon after we cleared the marina channel buoys, I unfurled the jib and cut the engine. Blissful silence and a beautiful afternoon. We were sailing on Boca Ciega Bay, in *Jacie Sails*'s new home...!

As we enjoyed the beautiful day and drank in our new semi-tropical surroundings, I fiddled with the electronic chartplotter gadget at the helm, and noted our depth, speed, and whatnot.

After a certain amount of time and distance, one tends to run out of water deep enough for the boat, so I decided it was time to tack.

And there's the rub.

The boat didn't seem to want to turn to the right. When tacking to port, everything worked fine; but when we tried to tack to starboard, we couldn't seem to get through the eye of the wind.

After a couple of aborted tacks, something occurred to me.

This is the same direction—to the right!—we had trouble turning when we left the fuel dock.

Hmmmmm.

Also, I remembered I'd asked Capt. David to bolt the propane locker back into place, as Electronics Guy had left it completely loose and banging around when he installed the autohelm tiller arm.

Hmmmmmmm.

Furthermore, the propane locker and tiller arm are both in the aft cockpit locker area, right next to each other.

Hmmmmmmmmm....

And did I notice a slight cracking sound as I forced the wheel as far right as possible?

Now, I may be slow, but I can see through a brick wall in time, as they say. I opened the port cockpit locker lid, and looked at the propane locker and tiller arm.

Yep. With the propane locker bolted into its proper place, it blocked the tiller arm from swinging all the way to the left side... which prevented *Jacie Sails* from turning more than just a hair to the right. Best of all, the fiberglass propane locker was now cracked from the tiller arm pressing into it.

No sweat. The locker's only job is to prevent a propane leak which could blow the boat into a billion tiny pieces. Any anyways, who needs to turn right...right?

Yeah, I was pretty pissed at Electronics Guy. He had obviously unbolted the propane locker because it was in the way of the tiller arm. But he didn't bother to mention any of that. Capt. David and I didn't notice the issue when I had him bolt the thing back in its original place, as the tiller arm happened to be swung over to starboard just then. Electronics Guy could have caused us to run into some nice expensive boats in the marina — or much worse. NOT. COOL.

At any rate, it was clear that we needed to fix this, so we dropped the hook (that new 35 lb. Delta, in fact) in front of the Gulfport waterfront, where we could bring Capt. David out in the dinghy and move the propane locker where it needed to go...and where also we could treat ourselves to a congratulatory beverage.

We hadn't visited the Gulf yet, but we had brought "our baby" to sunny Florida, given her some nice upgrades and repairs (or in some cases, snafus), and treated ourselves to a beautiful but challenging sail on Boca Ciega.

And by a major stroke of luck, hadn't racked up a large insurance claim.

21

FORCE YOUR SPOUSE TO GO

Don't worry if your wife (or husband, girlfriend, boyfriend or whatever) doesn't seem all that interested in sailing. They'll warm up to it in time if you just make 'em go with you on a regular basis.

~

Unless they kill you first.

The fact is, some folks just don't enjoy being wet, nauseated and bruised, and may even wonder what's wrong with you for wanting to go out and "enjoy" such things on a regular basis.

They may even question your decision-making for spending large amounts of money on your boat, as opposed to, say, fixing the roof. Or paying the rent. Or buying jewelry for your significant other on special occasions.

Nope, you've got to accept the fact that not everybody will grow to like cruising, and come to some kind of suitable arrangement. Otherwise, you'll just be one more couple on the rocks, figuratively speaking.

As my friend Captain Dan can tell you, it's amazing how many middle-aged men can be seen cruising south through the Caribbean with their wives, only to return north with a newer and younger model. Apparently a lot of wives decide that cruising is not for them, and their husbands decide that their wives are not for them, either. Not that that's ever happened to Captain Dan.

So maybe your partner will never come to love sailing like you do. But just maybe, if you approach the whole thing as carefully as you'd approach a spooked deer, you may be able to lure her in.

(It's usually the male of the species who gets the sailing virus first, but certainly not always. We'll stick with the statistical majority here. If you're going to bust my hump with political correctness, you're probably in the wrong community. Just sayin'.)

Exceptions abound, of course.

"My wife just sailed with me to the Caribbean," my friend Jim told me last month.

"Jamaica?" I asked.

"No, she wanted to."

Anyway, start out easy. Don't take your partner out on the Gulf during a small craft advisory. Try a protected lake or small bay in a light breeze. As it turns out, some folks tend to freak out when a sailboat starts tipping to one side, not realizing that it's what they're supposed to do. They may not enjoy walking around at an angle, trying to find things to hang on to and not fall into things.

Maybe you can just motor around a bit in light air, and throw a sail or two up just for looks. (Just remember to limit your time running downwind. There's nothing like smelling diesel fumes all afternoon to sour you on sailing.)

If and when your partner starts to find their sea legs, there are some things you can do at home to help acclimate them to the sailing life. (And best of all, these can be done as a couple.)

First, never dry your sheets entirely. Your partner can also occasionally climb into bed wearing damp coveralls and an overcoat. Second, try sitting on the washing machine — preferably after adjusting the feet so it wobbles a lot — while reading a book. (Like this book, for example.)

Finally, try cooking dinner on one burner while wearing heavy mittens.

~

Of course, it may turn out that there's nothing at all you can do to convince your significant other to love sailing as much as you do. Then you have a decision to make: Can you sail singlehanded, or do you need new crew?

But seriously, maybe your partner is into coastal and inland sailing, and you can find a friend or two for those ocean passages. Then your partner can fly in to wherever you end up.

And if in the end they're simply not into sailing, well...maybe it will be someone else's gain.

After all, that's how I ended up with *Jacie Sails*.

PART V

WHAT NOT TO BUY

22

WHO NEEDS TOWING INSURANCE?

Don't waste your money on frivolous things like towing insurance. Why would you even need towing insurance for a sailboat? You can always sail, right?

～

W ell, sure...but for one thing, folks usually frown on you sailing into your slip in a crowded marina. Particularly if the wind is light. Or heavy. But any time, really.

And there are a surprising number of times when having your engine kaput makes life harder on a sailboat.

Maybe you're wrapping up an overnight sail from the Keys and you're stuck twenty miles off Fort Myers Beach on a sweltering late summer South Florida day, in a flat calm which is predicted to continue for a couple of days, because you forgot to do something important with the water pump and part of the water pump pulley flew off and buried itself in the engine wall right next to where you sleep, and now you can't run the engine because you haven't learned yet to carry spare parts like fan belts. Not that that's ever happened to me.

Or maybe you're one of the first kind of sailor. (Those who've been aground, and liars.) And just maybe you went hard aground on the shallow area inside Marker 24 at Tierra Del Sol because you were in a hurry to make the opening of Structure E and weren't paying attention. That didn't happen to me, either. It was a friend of mine, you understand.

Maybe you're a slow learner like me, and you don't yet understand why, if you use your boat at all, you should absolutely make sure to get good towing insurance and pay it every year. (Or however often they want you to give them money.)

Let me just give you an example, then.

I just paid last month a whopping $161 to renew my annual Unlimited Gold membership with Boat US. Two days ago we had the cutlass bearing come out — which coincidentally happened right after I went aground and suddenly threw 'er into reverse — and we had to be towed about twenty miles back to our slip in the marina, a tow which would have cost us over a thousand bucks. It cost us zero. (But we tipped the towboat operator forty bucks cash. Don't be a cheapskate and give cruisers a bad name!)

Yes, we did the Tow Of Shame into John's Pass and down the ICW to our marina. Could we have sailed through the three drawbridges on a holiday weekend with very light wind?

Eventually, perhaps, if our sanity held out and the hundreds of drunk powerboaters didn't run us into a drawbridge and we didn't fire a flare gun at them and get arrested or something, then yes, we'd probably eventually get near the marina. At which point we'd still need to get towed in to our berth.

So towing is something that you're gonna become familiar with, if you actually take your boat out of the marina often.

Do be aware, by the way, that some towing policies are different than others, and there can be some gotchas. For one thing, you want to make sure the towing company or operator doesn't claim salvage on your boat. I'm not sure exactly what that entails, but it means the person coming out to "help" you ends up claiming that they salvaged your boat, and that it now belongs to them.

The two major providers, Towboat US and Sea Tow, shouldn't pose a big risk in this regard, but do your homework and be sure to read and understand before signing anything with the towing operator. (Be clear that it's a towing, and not a salvage, operation. I hear that has to do with whether your boat is taking on water or in danger of sinking or not.) I've been a Towboat US guy, and I've been very happy with them.

Also, some towing policies may cover towing from "out there" to the nearest place that can fix your boat, but may not cover towing from your dock to the same place. It's a weird little wrinkle, and the reason I have the Gold policy, which covers 100% of "dock-to-dock" towing.

I can't figure out how these companies make money with idiots like me out there, but I gather it's because so many people just don't go sailing enough.

23

EXPENSIVE ELECTRONICS UPGRADES

IT GOES without saying that you should have nothing but the best when it comes to electronics aboard, so just bit the bullet and go ahead and get the fanciest chartplotter you can afford, and make sure all your gauges from fuel level to holding tank level are tied in to it. Splurge on a radar, solar panels and a wind generator while you're at it.

There *are* some things that need fixing before you get out on the ocean. For instance, the seacocks on *Jacie Sails* that were part of the boat when we got her were nothing more than what you'd see on the spigot that goes to your backyard garden hose.

No bueno. In short, that will not do. Those things would have dropped off in a month or two in salt water.

On the other hand, there are things which you can maybe do without for a minute. And one group of these things is expensive electronics.

To be sure, good electronics can definitely make life easier and in many cases safer. At a minimum, it helps to know how deep the water is, and whether that number is uncomfortably close to the draft of your vessel.

If you decide that this cruising thing is indeed for you, then I think you'll really appreciate autohelm. And a VHF radio with AIS receiver and DCS calling is a beautiful thing. Okay, and I just realized the other day that radar can take a tiny bit of the pucker factor out of being stuck in the fog. (Although not all of the pucker factor.)

But here's the thing. As I may have mentioned, if you spend more than you can afford on your boat (including all the doodads thereon), you can't afford to go cruising. And you're not likely to enjoy it so much with all that debt hanging over your head.

And what if, god forbid, you decide that cruising's not for you? *No worries, all those gadgets will help the sale price*, you think. Poor soul. You may be a little too gullible to take up cruising at all, come to think of it. The value of all those fancy new electronic gadgets dropped faster than your car keys into the marina water the minute you walked out of the store with 'em. (Or more likely, told the boatyard to order while they're refitting your dream yacht.)

And another thing: the electronic version of the old fashioned gadget (whatever it is) is approximately 4.74 times more likely to fail than the old fashioned version. To be fair, research has shown that 97.3 percent of all statistics are made up, but I still find it to be true.

So while it may be damned handy to know how full the holding tank is simply by looking at your chartplotter, I have a more reliable and much cheaper method. I pull up the cushion in the v-berth, slide the wooden lid off the central compartment, and shine my headlamp, held in my hand, through the side of the translucent holding tank to see how full it is. Just to confirm, I may tap on the tank and listen to how it sounds.

I also pretty much know my fuel level most of the time via my own sophisticated method: I pull up the cushion on the quarterberth, unscrew the round plastic viewport, and shine my headlamp on the old-school fuel gauge fitted into the top of the tank.

The only times I've run out of fuel have been when *somebody* forgets to check the level. (I blame myself. I really do.)

My fancy engine temperature gauge consists of an "idiot light" on the panel on the side of the cockpit that lights up if the engine overheats, along with a buzzer — which I should probably fix, since it doesn't buzz any more, so I just have to keep an eye out for the idiot light or the smell of burning engine.

To be honest, though, not counting the fog episode last week and a few thunderstorms, the first thing I usually do when I boot up the electronics is to turn off the radar, which sucks power like a vampire at a hemophilia convention. And my fancy AIS function, which is supposed to tell me where all the big ships are, seems to work intermittently.

If you have a basic depth sounder and know how to read a chart, you actually could hold off on that fancy chartplotter for a bit. Heck, you don't even have to go old school with paper charts. You can get all manner of charts on your tablet or smartphone.

Once again, my attorney wishes me to say that handheld electronics are no substitute for proper charts, that you take full responsibility for listening to my drivel, and some other stuff I forget, because I was thinking about the new high-speed electronic whoozits I'm about to plunk down a wad of cash on.

24

EXPENSIVE RE-FITTING, IF IT'S NOT SAFETY RELATED

Now that you've got your boat out of the water, here is your big chance to add all of the things she could possibly dream of that you might need while underway. After all, you're probably never going to haul out again.

❧

Well, to be sure, I avoid haulouts like the plague, apparently. I have hauled out *Jacie Sails* one time since I moved her to the Gulf in 2013. And that was a mixed bag. Not because there was any damage involved in the haul out, but because the m—————— apparently couldn't fix a cutlass bearing for more than 100 miles worth of sailing.

So I'm trying to wait until the last minute (which is about two years ago) to haul out again.

I imagine that bottom paint's wearing pretty thin.

I did make some "improvements" after I trucked the boat down to Saint Pete.

I added a radar, which I have used several times since 2013. *Several.*

I fixed (excuse me, had somebody fix) the seacocks — and that situation was definitely safety related, because I hear it's a bad thing for the valves on your seacocks to corrode and suddenly come off while you're in the middle of the ocean.

But perhaps some "upgrades" aren't so necessary.

When I turn on my chart plotter, there are all manner of tempting statistics that I could be seeing, but which are showing up as a blank — or zero — on my plotter because there are no sensors to tell it what to display.

Why, I could actually know how much poop is in my holding tank at any given time! Of course, I can also just lift up the cushion on the v-berth and shine a light through the translucent holding tank. But still...that would be cool.

I can also have a better bead on how much diesel I have in the tank without having to lift up the cushion in the quarterberth, unscrew the little observation port and squint at the recessed fuel gauge in there.

OK, so that would be cool. But here's the thing (and let me put it delicately): it's just one more thing to f—, I mean, *mess* up.

And I've found, after several years in the salt water that things messing up tends to raise my blood pressure. Which tends to spoil the mood in my Little Zen Temple.

So I'm getting to be a big fan of simple.

As I may or may not have mentioned before, I highly recommend you check out *Sensible Cruising: The Thoreau Approach*, by Don Casey and Lew Hackler.

As they wisely point out, gadgets cost money. And the more money you spend on gadgets that you may or may not need, the less money you have to go sailing.

And did I mention? Gadgets tend to mess up. Heck, even the bulletproof type things on the boat tend to mess up, so let's not add any extra ones, shall we?

The one time I hauled out my boat after the initial refit, I'd purchased an hour meter, or Hobbs meter, to record engine hours. Which I hear is important. I had the resident electrical genius at the marina their install it in the cockpit just below the starter button. It lasted less than 100 engine hours before the water got in and stopped it. I believe I spent $50-$75 on that damn thing.

I had also been interested in trying to install a thermostat, analog or digital, to know the precise engine temperature. However, after a bunch of head scratching and brainstorming we ended up just keeping the "idiot light," and buzzer system that was there to begin with.

Of course, salt water has gotten into the buzzer (the second one I have installed), so now the only way I will be aware of the engine overheating is if I happen to notice the little red light next to the starter button. Or if the engine seizes up or catches fire or something.

If you see how fraught with peril even the simplest installations are, and how corrosive the effects of salt air and salt water, then you will realize how futile it is to install any extra crap that you actually don't need.

Now, there are some things that certainly make a lot of sense to have aboard. Like a propane sniffer in the bilge. There's nothing more disheartening to your daily routine than to be blown into a million tiny pieces because you had a propane leak into the bilge and didn't know about it until some random spark from your salty corroded electrical systems propelled you into kingdom come.

Also, a carbon monoxide detector is highly recommended.

Carbon monoxide is even sneakier than the propane, if that's possible. You lie down to take a nap, relying on your autopilot to navigate you through the shipping channel. (Just kidding. Don't do that.) And then you just don't wake up.

These two devices in particular also provide periodic entertainment, along with the high bilge water alarm, by setting off a screeching alarm at random times when they go bad. (Oh yes, you have to replace the sensors periodically. But you didn't actually want to spend time sailing, did you?)

Well, I have to run. I need to pore through a catalog to see about those dual cigarette lighters and high-speed hubcaps that I want to add soon.

25

EXPENSIVE OTHER STUFF (IF IT'S NOT SAFETY-RELATED)

OF COURSE you want to have the nicest-looking yacht out there, even if your budget is more "boat-y." Just put everything on plastic and West Marine will love you for it.

❧

I magine my surprise when I priced anchors at my local West Marine. The anchor I settled on, in galvanized steel, was $279.^{99}. The same size in stainless steel? 1,359.^{99}.

Just damn.

Okay, *that* decision was an easy one. (For me. I probably know people that have even less economic acumen than I do, who might convince themselves they can afford the stainless anchor.)

Honestly, I'm just not really a stainless kind of guy. Not on my budget. I'm also not a teak-varnishing kind of guy either, but that has more to do with wanting to sail instead of work on the boat.

Jacie Sails, I like to think, has that nice "well-used" look that discourages thieves and robbers. Not that she looks like one of those floating roach condominiums out in the bay. I just mean not everything is polished and varnished. (And given that she's a fiberglass boat, there's not a lot of wood trim to worry about, anyway.

But forget the outside cosmetic stuff for a minute. It can also be tempting to spring for a lot of other doodads that you may or may not need.

I would counsel you to practice some discipline here, and if it's not something essential to your safety, consider putting off that purchase at least until you know you're keeping the boat for a while, and that that doodad is really going to make your life better, and not instead introduce more problems and complications.

PART VI

WHERE NOT TO GO

26

THE FLORIDA GULF COAST

Why would you want to fool with Florida's Gulf coast? Isn't all the real action on the Atlantic? I thought all the cool kids were in Miami.

~

N o, and no.

Okay, I may be a little partial here. My home port is on the Gulf coast of Florida. But let me share a few things about the area that may convince you to check it out.

The Water Is Warm

Unlike the East Coast, the water in the Gulf is pretty tolerable all year long. (And compared to California waters, it's *really* tolerable.)

There's the Gulf Stream, for one thing. Or more specifically, the lack of it. Ironically, it doesn't pass the Gulf coast. So all that water sits around on the western continental shelf of Florida, getting nice and toasty. Bad for summer thunderstorms, but good for water temperatures.

During the summer, the water on the Gulf coast will be at least five degrees warmer than the eastern side of the state.

Over on the Atlantic side, I've always found the water to be pretty nippy at any time of the year. (Unless you consider the Keys to be part of the Atlantic side.)

Is it worth wading around in those chilly Atlantic waters, and the inevitable shrinkage that occurs, just to be trendy? I think not.

The Beaches Are Beautiful

I remember going to Daytona Beach. And no offense, but I can't imagine what people see in it. Unless your criteria is *Where can I get drunk and drive on the beach?*

The "sand" was more like concrete, packed hard by all the vehicles cruising the beach. *No bueno.*

Not to mention all the *people*. To quote a very thoughtful guy,

> "People are wonderful. I love individuals. I hate groups of people..."

> — GEORGE CARLIN

Okay, so there was a little more to it than that, but the whole routine was pretty funny.

I'm not saying that you'll find fewer people on the Gulf coast, because it depends on where you go. But it's a lot easier to find some elbow room on the west side of the state, compared to the continuous city that is West Palm-Fort Lauderdale-Miami.

Some of the most beautiful beaches in the world are on Florida's Gulf coast.

Siesta Key, near Sarasota, is consistently rated one of the best, due to its soft sugar-white sand. The same for Caladesi Island, near Clearwater.

There are some other beautiful (and even less-traveled) beaches on the Gulf coast.

Maybe if you listen to my *How Not To Sail* podcast, you'll hear about some of 'em. Just sayin'...

The Ocean Is Friendly (Mostly)

Besides being colder, the Atlantic is also rougher. Even though the Gulf Stream is several miles out, the eddies and countercurrents can make things ticklish at times, even near the shore.

With the easterly breeze the swells from the Atlantic have a nice long time to get going before they crash into Florida.

By contrast, the wide continental shelf on the west coast of Florida tends to keep near-shore conditions somewhat in check. The wavelengths are a little shorter, but overall conditions are better.

And don't forget that the shark attack capital of the world is New Smyrna Beach, Florida[1]. National Geographic says that anyone who has swam there has been within ten feet of a shark.

New Smyrna Beach is — you guessed it — on the Atlantic side.

Sure we get bull sharks, hammerhead sharks, blacktip sharks, tiger sharks and more in the Gulf. But if Nat Geo says the East Coast is more dangerous, who am I to argue?

The People Are Nice (Well, Relatively...)

Let's face it, Floridians are a bit more *abrupt* than other Southerners. And some of 'em are a little quirky.

There's a whole series of "Only in Florida" memes out there on the internet, for your entertainment. Just don't get the idea that *all* Floridians are folks who would start a fire and accidentally burn down a historic 3,500-year-old cypress tree because they were trying to see their meth better.

But regardless of the overall weirdness, I guess the Gulf Coast is a little more *southern* (and midwestern) and the East Coast is a little more *yankee.* Throw in a little latino *machismo* on the East Coast and you have a recipe for some fast-drivin', in-your-face kinda folks over there.

As you can tell, I prefer slower people, and less of them. Maybe I'm a little slow myself. But being from Atlanta, I feel like I can relate better to the Gulf Coast folks.

Southwest Florida

Okay, I have a confession to make. I may have to do a follow-up about the Florida Panhandle and Big Bend areas...because my experience in *Jacie Sails* has been mostly limited to St. Pete and points south.

Although like many good Georgians, we used to go to the "Redneck Riviera" on holiday (and despite my Dad buying a condo in Panama City Beach later in life), I haven't been to the Panhandle in a while.

I *did* have a nice visit with Eric Stone in Destin for the podcast a while back. And the beaches there looked beautiful...so I can see a Season Two coming up. But for most of this section right now, I'll be sticking with sailing destinations in Southwest Florida and the Florida Keys.

I find Southwest Florida to be really beautiful, warm, and in many cases, still nicely rustic.

There's a reason St. Pete is considered a sailing mecca. You have Tampa Bay right there, and a whole slew of great places to visit nearby, from Gulfport to Sarasota, Clearwater and more.

Further south you have Venice, Cabbage Key, Sanibel, Naples, and Marco Island, some of which I'll tell you about shortly.

(I'd love to be able to get into the Everglades, but with a five-foot draft, I can only pass by a few miles away in *Jacie Sails.*)

Finally, there are the Florida Keys (truly spectacular), including Dry Tortugas National Park. They're technically half-Atlantic, half-Gulf. But I'm gonna include 'em here.

First off, though, I want to tell you about one of the places I've been that's just *on the edge* of the Gulf of Mexico.

27

CUBA

DEFINITELY DON'T SAIL to Cuba...

~

B ecause I want it all to myself!

Note: If you're interested, you can see a cool video version of this chapter at HowNotToSail.com. Just search for "Cuba."

M ost of what you hear about Cuba is true. But it's not real until you go there yourself. It's a land of stunning beauty, great people and puzzling problems.

I sailed to Marina Hemingway from the Dry Tortugas with The Admiral in 2017, and most of what I read in various cruising guides and online did turn out to be accurate. But some things deserve special highlighting:

The Most Important Rules

- Rule #1: Bring toilet paper.
- Rule #2: Carry it with you at all times.

Toilet paper seems to be a nonexistent commodity in Cuba. I don't know what Cubans do when they don't have any, but I hear they use pages torn from the communist party newspaper.

And strangely, there are toilets but almost none of them have toilet seats. I imagine a vast and dusty warehouse somewhere in Cuba, piled high with toilet seats, which perhaps are doled out to farmers to use as collars for plow horses.

On the plus side, your quads will stay toned as you squat over the seatless toilets to do your thing. This cruising thing ain't for the weak.

I also discovered that (when we were there) the slip rates at Marina Hemingway were about one sixth of what we paid per night in Key West on New Years Eve. If you pay a modest fee to join the Hemingway International Yacht Club — and who wouldn't — ?you get a discount on slip fees.

> **Tip:** Be sure to join on your first day there and take the official letter straight to the harbormaster. Your discount won't begin until you take care of that. (Double-check me on this, though, since by the time we got to the Dry Tortugas and across the Gulf Stream, all I wanted to do was eat, drink, sleep and enjoy the good coffee at the marina snack bar.)

The "snack bar," by the way, actually sold coffee, rum and beer, and cigarettes. Plus they had laundry and bathrooms with showers. The Men's bathroom had a couple of showers that were not cold, and I used the five-gallon bucket from Jacie Sails to flush the toilet. The Women's bathroom had cold showers only when we were there, and I suspect nothing has changed. That may be less of an issue in the summer than it was in January during a cold front, which of course was when we were there.

Building Up Gradually

If you've been following for a while on Facebook, Twitter, Instagram, or in real life, you'll know I'd been sailing the Florida Gulf Coast and the Florida Keys since 2013, aboard *Jacie Sails*.

I built up gradually, making about a dozen longer cruises and a number of day sails. By the time we sailed to Cuba, I'd done over 3000 nautical miles. Over 2000 of those have were solo, and over 1000 were offshore.

But I had never sailed to another country.

Thankfully, I have a partner that enjoys sailing with me...and I haven't killed her yet, so she still trusts me.

And The Admiral, for some crazy reason, liked my idea about sailing to Cuba. In fact, we were going to go the previous year at New Years, but we couldn't figure out what damn papers and permits we needed.

What Documents You Need To Sail To Cuba

[NOTE: Political developments may may impact the legal requirements to be able to sail or otherwise travel to Cuba. Please plan accordingly!]

As a Captain, you'll need:

- passport
- visa (and if you're sailing, you get it at customs at the marina on arrival)
- US Coast Guard Form 3300 – Permission to Enter Cuban Territorial Waters
- "Ship's Papers"

- $29 DTOPS customs decal (this may be changing to a virtual permit)
- eligible "reason" for going (that is, you can't theoretically just go for tourism)
- certain vaccinations are recommended but not required

Now that's the simple version. *If you stay no more than 14 days, you can avoid some extra hoops with the US government.*

As a Crew Member:

Of course, if you're going there just as a crew member, all you really need is:

- passport
- visa
- your vaccinations (as applicable), and
- a legit reason to be there.

I'll tell you this: They're much more laid back on the Cuban side, in my experience. Don't bring any drugs or contraband, and don't f— up, and you should be good to go.

Final Plans

So anyway, we finally figured out what we needed, thanks to Linus from the Slow Boat to Cuba podcast and Captain Cheryl Barr's cruising guide; and Tanya booked a one-way flight to Key West.

I really wanted to go full ninja on this trip, documenting everything from a zillion angles like Matrix bullet time, and bringing every piece of video, photo and audio gear that I had — which is a considerable amount — but as it got closer to time to depart, I finally realized it might just be best if I focus on getting us from Point A to Point B and back in one piece.

The whole thing of getting these permits and decals and vaccinations and making sure the boat was ready to cross the Gulf Stream with minimal prep time was starting to weigh on me a little, and finally it was just time to *go*. I'd take a reasonable rig, focus on sailing the boat, and get to Cuba and back with a minimum of fuss.

St. Pete and Peter Suarez

After the usual Christmas festivities, I drove from Atlanta down to St. Pete on December 26th, arriving late at night as usual, and found the boat still afloat...which is always a good thing. I found my marina neighbor Peter Suarez aboard, and we may or may not have had a beverage once I got all the gear aboard.

If you're not familiar with Peter from HowNotToSail.com, he is one talented hombre. (Check out the hilarious "The Prisoner's Lament," performed by Peter and recorded by yours truly aboard Peter's yacht *Duende*.)

Don't cut that wire!

I had to leave on the 28th to meet The Admiral in Key West, so that left only one day to get provisioned and get money changed...which, as it turns out was largely a waste of time. I may elaborate later, but suffice to say changing US Dollars to Canadian Dollars to change to Cuban Pesos may not be necessary.

My friend Denis (the head honcho at Gulfport Marina) was kind enough to lend me his pressure washer to clean off all the birdshit so we'd look respectable, and on the 28th, the mad dash began.

Well, almost. It seems that a certain boatyard, when they installed tricolor running lights at the top of the mast, removed the deck level running lights from the breaker panel. I was *very* proud to be able to reattach the bow lights. But when I went to hook up a proper stern light, I mistakenly cut the wire from our solar panel that charges the batteries when we're away from the dock.

But I got that spliced and we were finally underway by late afternoon, in time to catch the sunset off Egmont Key in the Gulf of Mexico.

38-hour Nonstop Run (Well, almost…)

I motorsailed south all night along the Gulf Coast and finally lowered the main the next morning, since it wasn't bringing much to the party.

At Marco Island, I topped off the fuel, got some chips and junk food at Rose Marina, and kept on going.

I was able to set the main and jib leaving Marco, and left 'em up all night. Since we had a following wind, I didn't realize that it was getting pretty breezy until early morning on the 30th. Fortunately, I doused the sails and had a wet run down the Key West Northwest Channel just before dawn… A 38-hour solo run of 222 nautical miles.

New Years Eve in Key West

After I got tied up with the much-appreciated morning help of Corey at Galleon Marina, I caught a few winks before Tanya arrived.

We had planned to leave direct for Havana on New Years Eve, but the forecast wasn't great for the Gulf Stream, so we decided to hang out in Key West for New Years, then stop at the Dry Tortugas and wait for a good window.

The Galleon Marina was full the next evening, so we spent New Years Eve at the fuel dock at Conch Harbor Marina — which was also full, so we paid the same crazy $5 per foot "special event" dock fee that we paid at Galleon.

Still, it's hard to beat New Years in Key West; and we knew we wouldn't be paying any slip fees in the next few days.

We had our champagne toast early and totally missed whatever was going on at midnight.

The Dry Tortugas

On New Years Day just after dawn, we bid goodbye to family, friends, and the internet, and sailed — excuse me, motored — west to the Dry Tortugas.

Once we got a few miles from Key West, we were off the grid until we got to Cuba...and just barely on the grid once we got there.

Fortunately for our family and friends, we carry a Spot messenger so a few select folks can follow see our exact location track updated every 10 minutes, and we can also post manual position updates that show up on our Jacie Sails Facebook page.

Sink the Dink

There was one major issue we had to contend with: The dinghy hadn't been brought out and inflated in a good year, and it turns out it had a leak, so we didn't have a way to get ashore. Fortunately, the park rangers were very kind and let us tie up in the only remaining space behind the ferry for a couple of hours at a time. They even found us some repair materials and updated us on the forecast. Another sailboat also donated some potential patching material to try and make the dinghy buoyant again.

Unfortunately, the patch didn't hold, and we realized that the only way we'd be getting off the boat this trip was onto a dock or into the water...but meanwhile, Tanya was able to get some quality time on Bush Key. *[Bush Key is next to Garden Key, where Fort Jefferson is. The two are now attached by a sand bar. Ironically, Bush Key is where all the birds are — and "Bird Key" is now submerged.]*

Time to go...

As we checked in with the rangers on the morning of January 3, we saw from PassageWeather.com that our weather window had moved back to...now. We saw that during the evening, the Florida Straits was showing white on the chart, which means the wave height was forecast to be less than half a meter. That's about as good as it gets, so bidding a quick adieu and thanks to the rangers, we shoved off around noon.

We cruised by Loggerhead Key, with its lighthouse and beautiful beach, and headed south, crossing the southern boundary of the park at mid afternoon (14:28). A few minutes later, we reached the furthest point south that Jacie Sails has ever been; and by 16:30 we reached the deepest point that Jacie Sails has ever been.

The continental shelf on the Gulf Coast where I usually cruise is very shallow and extends out a good way, so the deepest point I'd been before was around 200 feet. The Florida Straits are another matter: at the deepest point, you are sailing with well over a mile of water below you.

As it turns out, though, the crossing south was a milk run. I swear it was smoother in the Gulf Stream than at either side. Leaving the Tortugas, we had 3 to 5 foot swells — which was no big deal, though, since they were long; and I mentioned to Tanya how different they were than the short chop on the Gulf Coast. We missed seeing the legendary purple water in the Gulf Stream, since we crossed the axis in the middle of the night...but we could live with that. The Gulf Stream itself, though, was really smooth — unlike on my way back!

We motored and put up the main, with the traveller all the way to port, so we were able to just catch the SE breeze in the main as we motored SSE, and between motorsailing and the Gulf Stream, we made 8 knots for a good while. In fact, we arrived so much earlier than the predicted 18 hours that we had to tack offshore and back until dawn, throttling down to maybe three or four knots, with Tanya and I reduced by fatigue to trading 15- and 30-minute tricks at the helm.

Are we burning?

Soon after I saw the lights of Havana, I noticed an acrid smell, like burning trash. I was afraid for a minute that it was the boat. But, as I found out later, apparently it *was* burning trash.

Near dawn, I noticed that a couple of targets which had been headed north on my AIS during the night were now headed south toward the marina channel marker, converging with us.

Oh HELL no. I pushed the throttle down a little until we were back up to 6.5 knots with no sail up. I'd be damned if we were going to be the last of three boats into customs and into a slip.

We galloped to the buoy and then eased off as we navigated the channel, which you do NOT want to stray from. As we turned to port, we met with a beautiful sight: Sunrise over palm trees, a pretty little cove...and the customs dock to port, right where it was supposed to be!

Checking In

Customs, thankfully, were fairly perfunctory. I think maybe it helped that we were the first boat of three that pulled into the customs dock in rapid succession. They did not take our flares or flare gun... although I'd read that they would. They didn't care about our couple of ribeyes, couple dozen eggs, cheese, etc....which I'd read that they would. Strangely, there WAS one senior-looking official who walked past us as we were docked; and his sole question was whether we had a drone aboard. Which in this case, we did not.

The customs guy was nice, patient with our language barrier, and when we messed up the form by switching the month and day in the American way, simply provided us with new ones.

He *did* ask me belowdecks near the end of the process and asked if I had any "gift," although he made sure to say it was not required. I gave him a copy of my CD *Guiro!*, which I hope he enjoys.

A female doctor in a white lab coat came aboard, took our temperature with a little infrared remote sensor, asked us a few questions about our travel, then left.

I (and then Tanya, one at a time) went into the little air-conditioned customs building with two computer stations and a spare seat in front of each. There was a small camera on a pole at each station, pointed towards the "guest" chair. I thought they were going to take our picture for some purpose; but I decided they were actually doing facial recognition to compare us to our passport photo.

A couple of minutes later, we were given visas and directed to Canal Uno, closest to the ocean...and we were in!

(Well, almost...we still had to talk to the dockmaster and the agriculture guy, but it was no big deal. There were one or two more requests for "gifts," they got us promptly hooked up to a new power pedestal, and once again we had air conditioning and....LAND!)

Marina Hemingway

Marina Hemingway is actually a few miles west of Havana harbor, which is pretty much reserved for cruise ship and commercial traffic. The boat slips at Marina Hemingway are comprised of four canals, each about a half mile long. We were on Canal 1, nearest the water, and there were maybe fifteen boats tied up on the south side of the canal; and none on the ocean side.

The rest of the canal was empty, except for a couple of unfortunate vessels at the east end of the canal that had seen better days.

Just a couple hundred feet west of us was the 24-hour "snack bar," which actually had coffee, rum, water, soda, bathrooms, showers and laundry. The Admiral and I went and got a couple of espressos every morning for $1 CUC each, which is somewhere around a dollar or a dollar and a quarter, if my math is right — and depending on how you change your money.

Fish to the Vapor with Garlic

When people ask how the food was in Cuba, the first thing I have to mention is that we ate chinese food and pizza pretty often, followed next most often by cuban sandwiches at the yacht club; and ham and eggs for breakfast at the little cafe on the east end of the marina. Obviously, none of these were serious local cuisine. We did eat about half a dozen times at local *paladares*, which are private houses turned into restaurants; and we ate lunch twice at El Templete, on the Malecon, overlooking Havana Harbor, which is pretty much a tourist area — and thusly, pretty nice. I got Tanqueray and tonic at El Templete, and The Admiral enjoyed the croquetas so much we had to come back. We enjoyed the *paladares* a lot, from fancy exclusive ones in Havana and Playa that our special contact got us into, to more regular joints in Jaimanitas, Santa Fe and Pinar Del Rio.

I know it sounds crazy that Marina Hemingway would have a chinese restaurant on the property, but that's exactly where we had our first lunch. On the second floor overlooking the entrance channel, it's a great place to catch some rays and chill out. Some of the English translations of Chinese dishes in a Spanish-speaking country were pretty interesting.

I did not try the "Fish to the Vapor with Garlic," but I assume it means "steamed."

The Land of Castro

People have been asking me, "What's it like down there in the Land of Castro? Are the cars all really those old Chevys?" There's so much to say, but the phrase that came to mind was: *good intentions*. People listlessly sweeping a weedy track at a school stadium that I never saw in use. Tennis courts at the marina with no nets, allegedly installed for Obama's visit. A big blank space that looked ready to be an outdoor basketball court, but simply contained a giant wooden chair.

The basic wage provided by the state isn't enough to get by, so everyone has to hustle. The folks running their own legit or black market businesses are friendly, ambitious and eager to please. The folks working at their state wage jobs are less enthusiastic.

We found the Cuban people to be very warm and friendly, resilient and good-spirited despite years of privation. There's a saying, you can get almost anything done, *if* you have the materials. But there's the rub.

Yes, there are a lot of Chevys, Fords, Packards and the like, from 1940s vintage to around 1960, I guess. The crazy thing is that every single one I rode in or saw up close had been converted to diesel.

There are also russian Ladas from the Seventies and Eighties, some newer chinese Geelys, and a few more common species for party officials or tourist rentals.

I'd say the amount of air pollution *per car* in Cuba is more than in the U.S. — both because most vehicles are diesel; and because most, whether diesel or gas, seem to be in need of a tuneup. Of course, there are far fewer cars here, even in Havana; and unlike, say, Atlanta, there's a nice trade wind to clean things up.

However, I was there for two weeks and had some sort of tickly-throat coughing issue almost the whole time, which is damned rare for me. It got bad enough to keep me awake one night after Tanya left. Maybe it was coincidence, maybe it was the air, but it seemed that some of the other cruisers and even some of the locals had a bit of a chronic cough. Maybe it was just something going around, who knows? Either way, it's not going to keep me from going back, but I thought it was worth mentioning it to my fellow #HowNotToSailers.

The climate was amazing as advertised, though. In January, the average temperatures are a high of 79° and a low of 61°. With a northern front, it can get chilly, which happened during our stay. More importantly, it gets especially breezy during the Northers, and you do not want to be out in the Gulf Stream. But it was still kind of fun to see Atlanta expecting snow while we were wearing shorts.

If you're planning on going, and need some advice, or can't figure out what you need or how to contact the marina, just hit me up. I know a guy.

28

CABBAGE KEY

No POOL, no pump out, no mall. Heck, they don't even have a deep fryer!
Why the heck would I want to visit Cabbage Key?

~

Because it's beautiful and the people are awesome, that's why.
Legend even has it that this is the place that Jimmy Buffet is
singing about in "Cheeseburger in Paradise." And I have no
trouble believing that.

I'd heard about Cabbage Key from my friend Todd, among others.
But I finally got to visit the place in August 2013, on my way to
Marathon.

And I was hooked from the start.

Cabbage Key, as folks like to say, is "a slice of Old Florida," with
spanish moss hanging from the trees, and not a paved road to be
seen. Located in southwest Florida at Mile Marker 60 on the ICW, it
sits just inside the barrier island Cayo Costa, in Pine Island Sound. It
is a shell mound, and one of the tallest spots in southwest Florida.

After pulling an all-nighter south from Gulfport (Florida), I
entered Boca Grande channel and then headed south again a short

four miles in the ICW before spotting the entrance to Cabbage Key to starboard. I had already raised Jeff the dockmaster on VHF, and he gave me perfect instructions for entry and helped me get tied up on the end of a T-dock. (Helpful hint for cheap boaters: Tipping is appreciated!)

It was a nice slow day, and I couldn't wait to get up the hill to check out the famous inn, which didn't disappoint.

> "After a long day on the water — let alone a long overnight — sometimes all you want to do is sit there and stare into space without being responsible for anything."
> –Your Humble Narrator

Sitting on the patio overlooking the docks, I was able to literally enjoy a cheeseburger in paradise while gazing out at *Jacie Sails*, along with "Floyd" the egret, and a number of ducks, turtles, osprey, racoons and more.

Now, there are a few things you won't find at Cabbage Key. The first thing you might notice is french fries. That's because there's no deep fryer on Cabbage Key, which is because there's no grease trap, which is because...well, I can't remember, but something to do with the environment.

You also won't find a pool or a mall, which means you won't find a ton of people, including little rugrats. Which is fine by me. In fact, the only ways to get to the island, if you don't have you own boat, is via the ferry or by helicopter.

What you will find are nature trails with plenty of nature; a water tower you can climb to enjoy a panoramic view of Pine Island Sound, Cayo Costa and the Gulf; showers and laundry (i.e., a washer and dryer); and a gift shop, where among other things, you can buy a "shower with a friend" towel or t-shirt. ("Shower with a friend" is painted on the outside of the boathouse where the showers are located — and I'm not permitted by The Admiral to say whether I've adhered to this instruction or not.)

And then there's the inn and bar, known both for great food and for the seemingly endless layers of signed dollar bills covering the walls and ceiling.

One of the most popular souvenirs at the gift shop is a t-shirt with answers to the Top Ten most asked questions, which are:

1. **70,000** (How many dollar bills hang on the ceiling and walls?)
2. **10,000** (How many float to the floor each year?)
3. **100 Acres** (How large is the island?)
4. **Cabbage Palm** (How was the island named?)
5. **Yes, we live here.** (Does the staff live on the island?)
6. **Marker 60** (Where on the ICW is the island located?)
7. **Potato Salad or Cole Slaw** (What kind of salads do you have?)
8. **Underwater cable** (Where does the electricity come from?)
9. **Well water** (Where does your fresh water come from?)
10. **Through the bar and to the left.** (Where's the bathroom?)

The current owner of Cabbage Key, Rob Wells, bought the island in 1976 and has a house right on the shore. I ran into Rob in the bar and talked a bit, and he sat with me for breakfast the next day and was kind enough to share some local knowledge using my iPad charts. Rob's a genuine and unvarnished guy, and tells it like it is. He seemed to think I was a little crazy to head to Marathon nonstop.

He might be right about the crazy part, come to think of it.

I was impressed enough by Cabbage Key to stop by again on my way home from Marathon, and couldn't wait to bring The Admiral to see this great new find. I've since been back a number of times, both solo and with Tanya — including several times for New Years Eve.

Every year, they do a New Years Eve dinner and costume party...which, um, I happen to have won twice! (Truth be told, that's all due to Tanya's expertise, but we don't want her getting the big head or anything...)

The short story is I love me some Cabbage Key. In fact, working with Rob's sons Ken (who has taken over many of the duties at Cabbage Key) and Robert (who runs Tarpon Lodge, another awesome destination nearby), I shot and edited a video for Cabbage Key.

I almost don't want to tell anybody about this place, so I can keep it to myself — but since you were kind enough to purchase this book, I reckon I can share it with you.

Enjoy!

29

DRY TORTUGAS

Of all the places I'd like to warn you away from, this is probably the most important. I really, really would like to make sure you stay away, and tell your friends to do the same. You wouldn't like it here. There's no cell service, no internet, no snack bar and no pool. Just don't come.

∿

I first visited Dry Tortugas National Park on Wednesday May 21, 2014, after a solo nonstop sail from St. Pete.

The Dry Tortugas are about sixty miles west of Key West, and the main feature is Fort Jefferson, on Garden Key. It's a huge fort, some 47 acres, built in 1847 and made out of 16 million bricks. It has seen very little action as a fort, and is mainly known as the place where Dr. Samuel Mudd was imprisoned, for tending to the medical needs of one John Wilkes Booth, the assassin of Abraham Lincoln.

The water in the Tortugas is as beautiful as the rest of the Keys; and since it's a national park, there's wildlife galore. There are lots of pelicans at the fort, and we saw showers of minnows boil out of the water as predators hunted from below. On one trip, Tanya spotted a grouper under the boat so big I had to convince her it wasn't a shark.

There are only two ways to get to the Dry Tortugas if you don't have a boat: either take the ferry from Key West, or come by seaplane. The seaplanes are pretty cool, taking off and landing right next to the Anchorage...or in some cases, right through it.

The Dry Tortugas are called "dry" because there is no fresh water to be found anywhere within the 101 square miles of Dry Tortugas National Park. There is no food or drink available once the ferry leaves each day, and there is no WiFi and no cellular service.

Which is just fine by me.

Tanya enjoys walking on the beach on Bush Key, and we both enjoy walking in and on top of Fort Jefferson. It's truly a magnificent structure, and I've gotten some great pictures from there.

You're required to anchor within a mile of the fort, and most folks anchor in the protected bight just east of the fort, between Garden Key, Bush Key, and Long Key. I've anchored there, and I've also anchored southwest of the fort. (Coincidentally right at one mile away, although it seems like you're right next to it.)

There's a little submerged key there, Bird Key, which I was hoping to be able to walk along in waist-high water. After passing back and forth over it in the dinghy, I was unable to find water shallow enough to stand in, but I'm sure I'd find it immediately if I tried sailing over it in *Jacie Sails*.

If there is *one* fly in the ointment (for cranky guys like me, anyway), it may be the few fishing boats that anchor in Bird Key Harbor most every evening and do god-knows-what for an hour or two before leaving. Okay, I know that doesn't sound like a problem, does it?

Well, the problem is that for the entire duration of these maneuvers, they leave their bazillion-watt bow spotlights on — which, as they are usually anchored downwind of the main anchorage, tend to shine right into your cockpit while you're enjoying supper. And as Murphy's Law would have it, if you anchor downwind of them, you can bet that one of the fishing boats will hook up stern to stern with another, and — you guessed it — you get the Apocalyptic Light Show anyway.

I don't remember this happening the first time I visited solo. I may have been too tired to notice. But when I took Tanya the following New Years, sure enough, just as we were settling in to dinner after a twenty-hour crossing, a mile southwest of the fort, a fishing boat came chugging in and anchored a hundred yards in front of us.

Nothing like diesel fumes with dinner.

Then their buddies arrived in a second boat and proceeded to tie up stern to stern with the first boat, and — apparently — begin to transfer their catch from one boat to the other. Or something.

You can see where this is going.

First, I went below and grabbed my own 12-volt spotlight and shined it at the offenders. Nada. Then I tried hailing them on channel 16: *The fishing vessel anchored in Bird Key Harbor, this is sailing vessel Jacie Sails...* Nada.

I tried the spotlight again and the radio, on various channels. Nada.

"I'll be right back," I said to Tanya, as she stared at me in horror. I climbed down the swim ladder to the dinghy, ripped the outboard into life, cast off the painter and roared off toward the fishing boat, leaving Tanya to wonder if she'd ever find my body. I was at that stage of anger where I begin to vibrate.

Reaching the joined sterns of the boats, I looked up onto the deck, where they had enough working lights burning to illuminate a factory floor. For a few seconds, the fishermen didn't see me at the edge of the light, what with their night vision being temporarily destroyed and all.

"I'd appreciate it if you'd cut out the spotlight," I said through clenched teeth to the first fisherman to notice me.

"Ees okay. We go soon," the puzzled fellow assured me, as he considered the strange angry bearded man in the inflatable below.

"Thanks."

Twisting the throttle, I roared off back to *Jacie Sails*. I'd rather they went ahead and cut the spotlight in the meantime. But at least they weren't going to be hanging around all night, and Tanya was relieved to see that she wasn't going to be stuck in the middle of nowhere with a disappeared Captain.

For the life of me, I still can't figure why these boats need to keep the bow spotlights on while they're anchored — and I'd love to see some kind of action on that (it's in a national park, for chrissakes). But for now, I just hope that you'll bear this in mind, and decide not to visit. At least while I'm there.

30

KEY WEST

So what's the big fuss about Key West? I'm not much of a party person.

∽

W ell, neither am I. Honestly "nightlife" and parties tend to annoy me. At least, until I get a coupla drinks in me. And I suppose that can happen to a fella in Key West.

And as far as I know, I'm not homeless (yet) or into the "alternative lifestyle," which make up two key demographics in Key West. (If you're gonna be homeless, you'd wanna be homeless in a great climate, right?)

But you can't skip Key West if you like history. Or a good harbor. Or a place to stop on the way from Florida's Gulf coast to...well, the Tortugas, Mexico, Cuba, Belize, the Bahamas, the Dominican Republic...you get the idea.

Way Cool History

Key West is *not* actually named because it's the westernmost of the Florida Keys. (It's not. That honor goes to one of the keys in Dry

Tortugas National Park.) Key West was actually named *Cayo Hueso*, or "Bone Key," by none other than Ponce de Leon, because of the white limestone rock formations he found there in 1521. (Also, it's said that the previous native inhabitants used the island as a communal graveyard[1].)

The only way to get to the island for centuries was by boat. Then in 1912, the Overseas Railroad opened up the island to regular land slugs — until the Labor Day Hurricane of 1935 destroyed that for a few years, being replaced by the Overseas Highway in 1938.

Maybe the isolation — and the fact that you still have to be determined to go there — account for Key West's rustic charm. But it is definitely different.

The Key West-ers are known as "Conchs" for some reason, and the "Conch Republic" celebrates their secession from the United States every April 23. No one can tell if they're really serious or not.

Key West is actually the southernmost city in the continental U.S., although the southernmost point is actually nearby Ballast Key. But you can still visit the big "Southernmost Point" marker at the corner of Whitehead and South streets.

And if you haven't been living under a rock, then you know that Ernest Hemingway called Key West home for years. You can even tour his house, which is still home to descendants of his six-toed cat.

President Truman (among many others) loved the island, and you can tour his place as well, which is now a museum.

It's easy to sea why presidents, famous authors, and even regular folks like Key West. The climate is temperate year-round, with a nice breeze, perfect for sailing.

You can find all manner of fishing from Key West as well, whether it's chasing marlin in the Gulf Stream or bonefish in the flats. Key West (like the Keys in general) is truly an angler's paradise. You don't have to be especially gifted to come up with dinner. Just make sure you have a permit.

A Great Place To Stop

I'll admit it, the place we usually dock in Key West, the Galleon Marina and Resort, is a little pricey. We've paid $5 per foot per night on New Years. (And good luck trying to get a slip at the last minute.) But we usually only stop for a day or two, and I'm usually ready for a little convenience after the long trip down from Gulfport.

I'm pretty fond of the little Sunset Tiki Bar at the Galleon, too. At least, that's what they tell me.

You can get a nice breakfast burrito or whatever you fancy at the little cafe on the east side of the Galleon and enjoy your morning while watching the charter boats prepare for their daily guests.

Speaking of which, even if you have your own ship, I highly recommend taking a sunset spin on one of the historic schooners in Key West, like the *Western Union* or the *Appledore*. They usually include beverages and some appropriate live acoustic music, and the guests are encouraged to help the crew hoist the sails and stuff like that.

The Admiral and I went on a sunset cruise early on in our relationship, and I blame — er, credit — that partly for the longevity of our relationship.

Of course, you have all the bars, like Hog's Breath Saloon and Sloppy Joe's. (Where rumor has it I played a gig many moons ago.) And Key West has a Hooters, so you know it's civilized now.

The Admiral and I really enjoyed watching the sunset from the deck at Louie's Backyard, on the south side of the island. Of course, it's pretty hard not to find a place on Key West where you can't enjoy the sunset!

But where usually end up visiting at least once, is the Schooner Wharf. Maybe because it's in easy walking distance from the Galleon.

Tanya loved the empanadas at Turtle Kraal, and it's really cool sitting there on the sidewalk overlooking the wharf. Or we can keep an eye on our boat from the upper deck of the Schooner Bar while enjoying the local music from the courtyard below.

What I'm omitting so far is that there's a popular anchorage in

"The Bight," just off the Schooner Wharf. You can anchor and take your dinghy to the wharf — and save plenty of doubloons, if you're a real cruiser.

I really should try that some time.

Boat Supplies Galore

Well, to be honest, I guess the only "chandlery" I've been to in Key West is West Marine. But that'll do if you need something quick, won't it? (Unlike so many boaters, I'm not going to bash West Marine just because they're the Amazon of marine supplies. They've always worked for me.)

Equally important, perhaps, you can also get groceries, toiletries and other stuff like that nearby, and dinghy it out to your boat. (Or if you're being fancy and staying at a marina, just cart it down the dock.)

Location, Location, Location

Just like the pioneers discovered, though, one of the best reasons to stop at Key West is that it's probably right on your way to somewhere equally cool.

Tanya and I stopped there on our way to Cuba. (We jogged over to Dry Tortugas in between, to wait for calmer weather, and the angle from Fort Jefferson to Havana proved to be a good one.)

My friend Victor pointed out to me that sailing around Key West is a lot less dicey than navigating the shallows north of Marathon, if you're the kind that thinks scraping the bottom on sharp coral heads is a bad thing.

So if you find yourself cruising Southwest Florida, you definitely owe it to yourself to check out Key West.

31

GULFPORT

*DEFINITELY DON'T COME **to Gulfport...***

∿

B ecause that's my home port. And the marina's already so popular there's a waiting list.

I like people well enough one or two at a time, but I don't need everybody and their brother coming to Gulfport.

By the way, I'm talking about Gulfport, Florida. Not Mississippi. Although if you go to the other one that's fine, too. Like I say, I'm not all that fond of people.

If you must come, though, you'll find an awesome little town tucked into the corner of Boca Ciega Bay next to St. Petersburg. It's nicely protected, particularly the marina, but you can get out into the Gulf of Mexico in about forty minutes at six knots. I guess that would explain their motto, "Gateway to the Gulf."

Jacie Sails has called Gulfport Municipal Marina home since 2013, and the folks there are awesome. Harbormaster Denis Frain has been doing great things both at the marina and the waterfront "downtown." The marina recently added a new building with a day room and new restrooms with showers.

Over on the city waterfront, Denis oversaw the addition of new floating docks and they're now adding small artificial reefs under the pier to encourage more fish and improve the water quality. Super cool.

Just next to the marina is Clam Bayou Nature Preserve, where you can enjoy nature trails with boardwalks that extend out onto the water, watch boats come and go from the marina, or just get your Zen on. I find it's a great little one- to two-mile walk from the slip in the morning or after lunch.

You can also rent paddle boards and kayaks from a vendor in the marina to explore the bayou and Boca Ciega Bay. Or if you're a stinkpotter, I suppose you can rent a pontoon boat or jet ski. There are also dolphin-watching and snorkeling powerboat trips most days to Egmont Key.

The city of Gulfport is a funky little place, with a vibrant art scene and plenty of quirky people. A friend of mine says that describes pretty much every little waterfront town in South Florida, but I still choose to think that Gulfport is a little special.

There are plenty of waterfront bars like O'Maddy's, Salty's and Neptune's. And just off the water there are a couple of gems, like Stella's cafe, with their great breakfast menu, and Tanya's favorite, Pia's Trattoria. We can't visit Gulfport without visiting Pia's for some incredible Italian food, crisp and clean with fresh ingredients, many sourced locally.

There are great events like the annual Gecko Ball and the Grand Prix, as well as the regular monthly First Friday and Third Saturday Art Walk, where artists, vendors and musicians line the sidewalks along Beach Boulevard.

There is also the Gulfport Casino, which seems to be a source of confusion to outsiders. In Gulfport Florida (and in the area), "casino" means something akin to "community center," not "gambling establishment."

The bright turquoise casino hosts dances, weddings and other events, and is also where the downtown docks are. You can pull up to the dock (or bring your dinghy to the dinghy dock) and stroll across the street for some food and beverage.

I still have to laugh remembering how Captain David insisted on making sure we got back safely to our dinghy from Salty's — as if *that* were the part of the trip where we were most likely to have a tipsy accident.

Anyway, like I say, don't come here. But if ya do, tell 'em Bradford Rogers sent ya.

32

SANIBEL

WHY THE HECK would you wanna go here? There's not even a single high-rise condo on the whole island.

~

Okay, so maybe I've already made my point on this one. The Admiral and I first discovered Sanibel in 2015 on our way to the Florida Keys.

If you look at a map of Southwest Florida, Sanibel is the elbow that sticks out just above Fort Myers Beach and Naples.

One of the cool things about Sanibel is that when the city incorporated in 1974, they drew up the Sanibel Comprehensive Land Use Plan, which basically protected Sanibel from looking like...well, most of the Florida coastline.

Almost two thirds of the island is a nature preserve, and building codes for the remaining third of the island are strict.

Sanibel is home to a vibrant variety of animals and plants. Nearly three hundred confirmed species of birds have been spotted on Sanibel, along with twenty-two species of mammals (counting humans), fifty species of reptiles, and more than a thousand species of fish in the waters around Sanibel[1].

I didn't know what to expect when The Admiral booked a slip for two days on the island. But since she's been game enough to sail around with my crazy ass, I figured I should probably humor her.

The leg from Gulfport down to Sanibel took over twenty hours, but since it was the first day of our cruise, we had plenty of energy. Well, okay, *enough* energy. We were off Anna Maria Island by dinner time on August 22, and made it down around the outside curve of Sanibel, back up into San Carlos Bay, and to the marina (on the inland side of the island) by noonish on the 23rd.

The entrance to Sanibel Marina is narrow, and there were only two slips, if memory serves, able to accommodate *Jacie Sails*. So the marina isn't visited so much by a lot of our sailing friends.

In fact, the island isn't visited by too terribly many people at all, thanks to the aforementioned lack of highrise lodging and garish tchotchke shops. Which is just fine by me.

Tanya and I got tied up in a slip, and immediately limped a couple hundred feet into Gramma Dot's restaurant for something unusual: equal servings of water and beer. ('Tis true, my friends.)

I believe it was a very warm day. Also, I weighed about thirty pounds more than I do now. But I felt like I'd sweated at least five pounds off that day.

The following morning, Tanya and I walked out of the marina and down the road to visit the beach and the lighthouse. It was again warm.

Sanibel has over 65 miles of trails and walking/biking paths, and the walking path from the marina down to the lighthouse and beach on Ybel Point is a great walk. There are all kinds of trees and flowers I can't identify, and as you walk along the two-mile stretch you'll undoubtedly be serenaded by the songs of a dozen different bird species — which I also can't identify. But I'm working on it.

The beach is a great place if you like shelling. Because Sanibel kind of sticks out into the Gulf of Mexico, its beach collects a *lot* of shells. (And the occasional shark tooth, I hear.)

Did I mention it was warm that day?

So after giving The Admiral her required beach time, we sauntered back up the nice paved walking path toward the marina. And I was melting into my shoes. My shirt and hat band were drenched with sweat.

As we passed the only "commercial" section of our walk (consisting of maybe three or four fairly tasteful shops), Tanya suggested we duck into the Lighthouse Cafe for some brunch. I wasn't very much into the idea, but my debating skills were not at their peak.

So we went in...and boy am I glad we did! We enjoyed an excellent brunch of coffee and grapefruit and...well, whatever the hell else I ordered. But it was good, I tell ya.

Tanya bought some Lighthouse Cafe jam as well, which I have to say was very tasty. We need to visit and get some more soon.

In the evening, we chilled on the boat and watched a pretty serious lightning show over Fort Myers. Unfortunately, it was a precursor of what was to come soon on this trip...but that's a story for another time. (see "Lightning Is Overrated")

33

UNCLE HENRY'S MARINA

WHAT KIND of name is Uncle Henry's Marina, anyway? Is that a real thing?

~

W hy yes it is. And it's a really cool hidden gem on the north side of Gasparilla Island in Southwest Florida.

We found Uncle Henry's because Boca Grande Marina on the south end of the island was full. (And, I'm just gonna guess, a little more expensive.)

Uncle Henry's Marina is nestled at the southwest end of the channel between the Boca Grande Causeway and the spur of an old railway bridge, from which the center span over Gasparilla Sound and the ICW has been removed.

We contacted the harbormaster on VHF when we got to the channel, and he told us to proceed down the channel and call him back shortly for more instructions.

The channel is a mile and a half long, narrow and twisty, with a particular jog northwest at one point, so pay close attention to those instructions.

The old railway spur next to the marina is now used as a fishing pier by the locals, and I enjoyed going over there and getting my photography on.

The marina office is on the third floor of the marina building. All the better to keep track of rookies like me entering and leaving the channel.

I may or may not have run aground right in front of a law enforcement officer as we were leaving the channel, by failing to notice which side of the twisty markers I was on. I'm sure the folks fishing on the railway pier were laughing their asses off. It's enough to make you spill your drink.

Past the marina office is Kappy's Market, where you can also rent a golf cart to explore the island.

Funny story: I rented a cart to head down into Boca Grande with Tanya. She wanted to have lunch at the Pink Elephant, which we did. It's a little swanky, but I think the food was good.

At a table nearby, a group of well-to-do young folks was clearly having a large time. As we were wrapping up, three guys from that table took their leave, got into their golf cart, and promptly backed into our rented cart.

I immediately popped up like a meerkat from our patio table to make sure the driver saw me, and said something. I have no idea what.

"No worries, it's okay," he assured me from the road. Like a sucker, I believed him.

As they sped off, I went to check on our cart. Sure enough, the trim around one of the headlights was messed up, and it looked like we'd be paying some money to the rental place.

Thankfully, one of the ladies from the same group took pity on us — or perhaps decided her male friend was an asshole or something — and actually gave us the fella's cell number.

Tanya and I retreated back to Kappy's, where we confirmed that, yes indeed, somebody needed to pay for the damage to the cart. It may have been possible just to return the cart, and maybe nobody would notice for a while, but we didn't fancy that approach.

After a brief back and forth via text, culminating with my offering to call the authorities to report a hit and run, our intoxicated friend said he'd bring me some money. I paced back and forth at Kappy's until he arrived with enough cash to satisfy the rental person.

Just another day in paradise.

Ah, but where was I? Anyway, Uncle Henry's is a narrow marina, basically one dock that stretches out from the marina office towards the channel, nestled between the old railroad pier to the southeast and some two-story condos to the northwest. It has a nice, homey feel to it, and as I recall was fairly quiet. (A big plus in my book.)

And if you don't have any misadventures with golf carts, there's a good chance your stay will be enjoyable.

So if you're looking for a place to stay on the north side of Gasparilla, look up Uncle Henry's...and tell 'em Bradford sent ya. That ought to confuse them.

PART VII

PEOPLE NOT TO MISS

34

BOB BITCHIN

WHAT COULD you learn from this guy, anyway? I mean, he's a biker, for Pete's sake. He readily admits he's a three-time failure at business, and even that he's not the sharpest tool in the shed when it comes to sailing. Heck, he doesn't even look like a sailor. (Okay, maybe he does look like a pirate, though.)

∾

W hy would I include Capt. Bob Bitchin here?
Because he ruined my life, that's why! It's actually one of Bitchin's catch phrases: *Another life ruined.*
In fact, I have to watch that I don't steal any of Bob's funny sayings and similes, because (a) they tend to stick in your head, and (b) you don't want to piss off a three hundred pound tattooed biker who used to be Evel Knievel's bodyguard. (Look that up if you're under forty.)

Over the last three decades or so, Bob has ruined an untold number of lives via his books, *Latitudes & Attitudes* magazine, Latitudes & Attitudes TV, "Share The Sail" events, his new Pyrate Radio show, and so much more. He's become *the* ambassador of the cruising lifestyle.

My path to ruination has been serendipitous, but it has Bitchin's bad influence written all over it.

When I visited the Florida Keys in 1997 to get my scuba certification — and even more when I went back again to play some gigs in Key West in 1999, something bit me. The ridiculous turquoise water. The warm sun and beautiful clouds. The Trade Winds.

I can't pinpoint exactly when I started getting the cruising bug, but I can pinpoint some of the culprits. And Capt. Bob Bitchin is probably the main offender.

I started subscribing to Bitchin's magazine at the time, *Latitudes & Attitudes*. And it was an eye-opener. It wasn't about the coolest new spinnaker material, or who was doing what in the latest yacht races.

It was simply about what it was like to be *out there*.

From columns by Tania Aebi and Woody Henderson, to the mouth-watering pictures and stories submitted by folks around the world (okay, mostly in the tropics, which is fine with me), to Bitchin's own editorial at the beginning of each issue and the whole sensibility of his magazine, this was a publication all about getting out there and enjoying life on the water — preferably in a blow boat.

And I loved it. I even wore my L&A "The Floggings Will Continue Until Morale Improves" t-shirt when I played the Atlanta Jazz Fest in 2008 — which apparently didn't sit well with the deputy mayor. (I'm sure she's a fine person...but not much of a sense of humor, let's just say.)

I first met Bob at one of the St. Pete boat shows maybe in 2011 or so, but I didn't hang out. I just wanted to have a look and shake hands with this crazy man that had gone from biker to sailor. (And, um, he may even have a book about that.)

Ironically, I believe I was that very same trip scoping out Gulfport Marina as a possible home base, even before I had a boat.

And then, a few years ago, Capt. Bitchin had what you might call a "setback."

Some nice folk offered to buy Latitudes & Attitudes, which would allow Bob (and Jody, his more attractive half) to spend more time sailing.

Suffice to say, they took Bitchin for everything he had (including the magazine and everything associated with it) and left him holding the bag. The short story is the "buyers" ran up all of the L&A credit cards (over half a million dollars), took all the income for several months without paying the bills, and buggered off to South America.

Now, a lesser man might have folded here. One might even expect a former biker, bodyguard and generally large fellow to eliminate the cheats with extreme prejudice.

But (thankfully) what Bitchin did, with the help of some of the awesome L&A family, was to rebuild. Using the previous name was not an option at the time, so *Latitudes & Attitudes* was reborn as *Cruising Outpost*.

At first, I wasn't aware of this good news. I wondered why L&A had disappeared, but it was like it had just vanished. At the same time, I was — finally! — in the final throes of getting ready to buy a boat and go cruising. So I had pretty much taken an axe to anything that resembled a subscription, and wasn't looking for any more.

Turns out that the same month I found *Jacie Sails*, Bob and his merry crew were putting out the first issue of *Cruising Outpost*. As Bitchin might say, *How kewl is that?*

And the good news is that *Latitudes & Attitudes* is alive and well again, both in print, and on LatsAtts.com. (I highly recommend it, and have taken the very unusual step of subscribing to the print version, which also includes online access. There's just something about having a print magazine full of awesome photos to set your margarita on. Just sayin'...)

Fast forward to this year, and I reached out to Bob as I was preparing this very book you're reading right now.

I was planning the podcast and website (HowNotToSail.com), and had nothing more in mind than, "I wonder if Bitchin would give me a crack at a column or something."

I assumed if I emailed, I'd get some gatekeeper telling me to have a nice day — and in fact, I was kind of dreading it for that reason. But the whiteboard in my office kept staring back at me, with "How Not To Sail" as the only remaining item on it.

So with a shrug, I drafted an email to Bob with a couple of links to my Cuba podcast and to a draft "How Not To Sail" video episode (currently still guarded by monks at a secret monastery in the Upper Fendi).

Lo and behold, not only did he email me back within half an hour...he said he liked my stuff! We've pretty much got the columns covered, he told me, but I may have some other ideas for you.

To make a long story a little shorter, among other things, Bob introduced me to Capt. Dan Horn, from Pyrate Radio. And that led to a radio show on PyrateRadio.com, and now the *How Not To Sail* podcast.

Just to square the circle, I got to hang out with Capt. Bitchin (and Dan Horn and Eric Stone, and a bunch of cool people) at the St. Pete Power & Sail show...only this time, to plot new ventures and adventures.

And this time, I drove over from *Jacie Sails*, just fifteen minutes away.

Now *how kewl is that?*

∾

You can find part of my interview with Bob Bitchin in Episode 1 of the How Not To Sail Podcast *at HowNotToSail.com/1, or wherever you listen to your favorite podcasts.*

35

BERNARD MOITESSIER

WE ALL KNOW that the French can't write so good. And they're so damned arrogant. And it's not like Moitessier did much of note, anyway, right? So why bother reading this tripe?

~

Okay, so maybe the french *are* arrogant. But that's okay...so am I. And along with *Latitudes & Attitudes*, Moitessier's book *The Long Way* played a major role in stoking my cruising addiction.

What Saint-Exupéry did for flying, Moitessier did for sailing. Beautiful writing that makes you fall in love with the sea, and all its beauty and remorseless power.

At least, that's the case with *The Long Way*.

My neighbor Capt. Peter Suarez was telling me about reading *Sailing To The Reefs*, or one of Moitessier's other books. He wasn't blown away.

"No, no, you're totally reading the wrong one! You've got to check out *The Long Way*," I said. (Okay, maybe I'm sounding like a Frenchman myself now.)

But if you're not familiar, a little background.

Back in 1968 — when I was barely a toddler and before men had landed on the Moon — a group of crazies were planning what back then was a cool new extreme sporting event.

Joshua Slocum had been the first to sail solo around the world in 1898 (and in tribute, Moitessier named his boat *Joshua*), but that trip had taken over three years. In the intervening seventy years, sailors had gradually upped the ante, but still nobody had ever gone around the globe "solo, nonstop and unassisted."

If you're reading this, you probably already appreciate what a big deal that is. But if you're not sufficiently blown away, just consider some of the "little wrinkles" involved in pulling this off in 1968:

- Alone at sea for over 10 months
- No weatherfax to warn of approaching storms
- No engine
- No GPS or satellite beacon
- If and when you sleep, anything can happen
- Sail changes in a storm are your problem
- You can't pull into port for repairs, or you'll be disqualified
- No long range radio (for Moitessier)
- Icebergs (enough said...just think *Titanic*)
- Eating crappy canned 1968 food for 10 months. Not awesome!

Anyway, a small number of sailors were independently toying with the idea of going around alone and nonstop, but they were all pretty much aware of each others' preparations and of course all wanted to be the first to do it.

When the British *Sunday Times* newspaper got wind of this, they organized a prize competition. The rules were simple: Start and end in England, by passing south of the three "great capes," Cape of Good Hope (Africa), Cape Leeuwin (Australia) and Cape Horn (South America). The first sailor to make it around solo, nonstop and unassisted would win a golden globe trophy, and the fastest time would win £5,000.

Moitessier of course disdained what he considered a bastardization of the competition by the paper — but managed to participate anyway. He refused to carry a radio, considering it an "intrusion," but took along a film camera and a slingshot, from which he could periodically launch film of his trip and logbook at passing ships.

I shit you not, dear reader. And if you think that's unusual, there's more where that came from.

You see, having completed around three quarters of the race — and having passed the last major challenge, Cape Horn — Moitessier got a bug up his ass. Although he was in good position to win the competition (whether he knew it or not is unclear), he decided...to keep sailing.

Instead of heading up the Atlantic toward the finish line, Moitessier crossed the South Atlantic back to Africa, and drew near the Cape of Good Hope again just long enough to slingshot a message advising the *Sunday Times* (and notably not his family), *I am continuing non-stop towards the Pacific Islands, because I am happy at sea, and perhaps also to save my soul.*

Yeah, he was quite a hoot, that Moitessier. He ended up circling the globe another half lap, landing in Tahiti, where he penned *The Long Way*.

Now, the actual story is pretty interesting to begin with, but the book is...breathtaking. I don't know what the original French translation is like, but the prose in my English version is refreshingly spare, but descriptive. Without needless asides, Moitessier brings us the wonder of *being out there*.

But there's no way I can do justice to Moitessier's writing by writing about it. It's something you have to experience for yourself.

The long and the short of it is that *The Long Way* is another reason for my current "sailing problem." It not only added to my love of the sea, but also got me interested in other sailing adventurers and their exploits. (For a while, I was even enamored of the whole solo long distance sailing thing...but I recovered my sanity once I tried it a little.)

Since I first read *The Long Way*, I've sailed about a thousand miles a year, along the Gulf Coast and the Florida Keys, to the Dry Tortugas and Cuba, racking up a few solo passages of a couple hundred miles at a time. (Of course, unlike Moitessier I have autopilot, a satellite transmitter, VHF, an engine, and have never been far from potential rescue by the Coast Guard.)

And I've decided there's one thing that I won't be doing,: A solo nonstop circumnavigation like Moitessier.

Cojones grande, indeed. And maybe *un poco loco*.

As an interesting aside, I just discovered in Bob Bitchin's new book Biker to Sailor *that Bitchin was present for a freak storm in December 1982 in Cabo San Lucas that beached Moitessier's sloop* Joshua *along with twenty-two other boats. Bitchin safely got the hell out of the anchorage at the last minute in the original Lost Soul.*

Moitessier managed to get Joshua *off the beach, but sold her for a token amount and returned to Europe to write his autobiography.*

36

ERIC STONE

So what in the heck is a musician doing in this section? And what's with this "Trop Rock" stuff, anyway? I'm not a big Jimmy Buffett fan.

Well, neither was I. But it's growing on me. And I attribute that to a couple of things: My stint on Pyrate Radio as affable dunce Captain Billy Shine, and getting to know Eric Stone and his music.

And for that, I can circle back to blame Bob Bitchin.

Way back in the Stone Age, Eric brought a demo of some of his music to Bob at one of the zillions of boat shows Bob's attended. (I want to say Chicago was the venue.)

Before the weekend was out, Bob knew he had something "very kewl" on his hands. And it wasn't long before Eric's CDs were featured in every issue of *Latitudes & Attitudes* magazine.

That's where I first noticed Eric. But I'm a stubborn fella. *I don't buy stuff from magazines*, I figured. *I'll just flip over to the cruising photos.*

It wasn't 'til later that I actually heard one of Eric's tunes. And guess what the title was?

You see, at some point, Bob and company (I think Eric was in on this powwow) decided to start Latitudes & Attitudes TV.

Once again I was stubborn. (Or slow. Your call.) In the dusty recesses of my brain, I'd noticed some ads for Latitudes & Attitudes TV in the magazine. But it wasn't until Season Four or so that I actually searched and found it on one of our cable channels.

"Hey, look!" I said to The Admiral. "You gotta check this out."

Tanya was skeptical at first, but I think she liked the show. This was just before I got *Jacie Sails*, if I recall.

Anyway, the theme song for the show, one that invaded your brain and stayed there on infinite loop, was a song by Eric Stone, called...

Latitudes & Attitudes.

It fit the whole vibe of the cruising lifestyle perfectly, and made me want to jump up and grab a coldie and go sailing some place warm. (I did jump up and grab a coldie, but that's just because the other one was empty.)

And if you're not already familiar with "Trop Rock," that's pretty much what it's about. Trop Rock is a celebration of the boat and the beach. And the beverage.

You may be familiar with one of Trop Rock's most famous artists, and you probably either love him or hate him. That would be Jimmy Buffett.

I confess that my thoughts on Buffett's music for a while were...*meh.*

But the more time I've spent aboard *Jacie Sails*, the more I get it. Trop Rock is feel good music, and folks that listen to it sure seem to be enjoying life, no matter what sort of silly things they do when the tribe gets together.

As BeachfrontRadio.com says:

Tropical Rock, commonly referred to as "Trop Rock," is a genre of music that blends other genres including Rock, Reggae, Country, Caribbean and Latin with an island, tropical, beach musical arrangements and/or laid-back lifestyle lyrical themed songs.

Although Trop Rock has its roots in the beach music scene from the 60's, Jimmy Buffett is often credited as putting Trop Rock "on the map".

Crossover music stars like Kenny Chesney, Zac Brown and Jack Johnson have brought the Trop Rock music genre into the mainstream public, resulting in a growing popularity that has opened the door for a whole new generation of island-inspired musicians[1].

But Buffett is an outlier. The true rise of Trop Rock came when Pro Tools and Napster and other cool technologies began to allow musicians with shallower pockets to record and distribute their own original music. (It feels like this was in the late 1500s, but I guess it was in the 1990s.)

Although many acts like Zac Brown Band and Kenny Chesney feature full band production, many popular Trop Rock songs are recorded with bare bones production, either using programmed backing tracks or straight-up acoustic guitar and vocals, sometimes recorded at live shows.

This DIY mindset and thriftiness — and the appetite of fans for uplifting tunes, with or without expensive production — allows talented songwriters and performers in the genre to survive and thrive.

And Eric Stone is one of the best.

Based on my experience, Eric averages around 735 live shows per year[2]. For many of those he performs solo on acoustic guitar and vocals, and for others he may employ another guitarist or percussionist.

Watching one of these gigs is like watching Shiva on roller skates. He's up there like some kind of multilimbed deity, stomping on foot pedals, broadcasting live video, cueing up the next backing track on his iPod, and taking requests and chatting with fans on his iPad. Somehow it all works, and fans travel from all around to see him.

Which is also one of the hallmarks of the Trop Rock tribe. They like live music. They like getting together with other members of the tribe, over a cold beverage, preferably in a warm climate — or at least one near the water.

And if you're in the mood for some mental sunshine and sand, Eric Stone's music is a great place to start.

(And I'm not just saying that because he let me sit in on a live video jam a while back.)

So if you aren't familiar with the Trop Rock genre — or with Eric Stone — just turn on some of his music next time you're on the boat. Or somebody else's boat. Or in your back yard with your feet in the plastic pool with a Pabst Blue Ribbon in hand.

You'll thank me.

You can find part of my interview and jam with Eric in Episode 8 of the How Not To Sail Podcast *at HowNotToSail.com/8, or wherever you listen to your favorite podcasts.*

NOTES

10. Don't Bore Me With Rules

1. Based on Wikipedia: "Lighthouse and naval vessel urban legend."

26. The Florida Gulf Coast

1. http://natgeotv.com/ca/human-shark-bait/facts

30. Key West

1. https://en.wikipedia.org/wiki/Key_West

32. Sanibel

1. *Living Sanibel: A nature Guide to Sanibel & Captiva Islands.* Sobczak, Charles. ©2010 by Indigo Press, LLC.

36. Eric Stone

1. https://beachfrontradio.com/trop-rock-artists
2. A recent study conclusively proved that 94.78% of all statistics are made up.

ALSO FROM WORLDSONGS MEDIA

Books and things by my Dad,

Ray B. Rogers

Depression Baby:
True Stories from Growing Up During the Great Depression in Appalachia

(Kindle/Paperback/Hardcover/Audiobook)

Up From Hanging Dog:
When you're born in Hanging Dog, the only way to go is up!

(Kindle/Paperback...audiobook coming soon!)

All available at DepressionBaby.com

The Depression Baby Podcast

RayBRogers.com/podcast

ABOUT THE AUTHOR

Bradford Rogers is a musician, producer, voiceover artist, alleged sailor, and host of the *How Not To Sail* podcast.

Since buying the boat now known as *Jacie Sails* in 2012, Bradford has sailed over 6,000 miles in 'er and hasn't killed anybody yet...as far as you know.

We highly recommend you ignore any of his so-called "nautical advice."

facebook.com/hownottosail

twitter.com/hownottosail

instagram.com/hownottosail

youtube.com/hownottosail

Made in the USA
Coppell, TX
28 January 2021